KERNEL TWO

STUDENTS' BOOK

Robert O'Neill
with listening practice contributions by
Claire Woolford

Longman

Longman Group Limited
Longman House
Burnt Mill
Harlow, Essex/CM20 2JE, England
and Associated Companies throughout the world.

First published 1982
Eighth impression 1987
ISBN 0-582-51642-0

Illustrated by Ann Baum, Peter Dennis, Chris Evans, Charles Front, Maggie Ling, Geoffrey Tristram, Technical Art Services

Cover photograph by The Image Bank

Printed and bound in Spain by TONSA, San Sebastian

Acknowledgements

I wish to thank first of all the two teams of advisers for this Students' Book:

Author's Team
Alan McLean
Muriel Higgins
Claire Woolford

Editorial Team
Tim Hunt
Judith King
Joy Marshall

Their valuable cooperation was instrumental and decisive in the final design and contents of this book.

In addition I wish to thank the many fellow teachers and students who gave me help, formal and informal, with various aspects of this book. Most prominent among these are:
Rosalyn Hurst, Gareth Thomas, Frank Steele, Jean Borreye, Sue O'Connell, Aniko Pustaz, Peter High and various groups of learners at such places as the English Language Centre in Hove, the Volkshochschulen in Munich, Stuttgart and Neu Biberg, and classes of adults and older teenagers in Portugal, France, Italy and Spain.

I should also like to mention Tony Thorne, who did the artwork for the pilot versions of the book.

Finally I wish to thank Mr Ehrhard Waespi, Director of the Eurocentres, for his continuing support, advice and encouragement.

Robert O'Neill
London 1982

Contents

Unit One

A

Claire Walton and the television programme *The News in Focus*.

1

Good evening. This is Claire Walton with *The News in Focus*. This evening, as always, we look at some of the stories behind the headlines in the newspapers.

COMPANY DIRECTOR DIES IN FACTORY FIRE
THOUSANDS SEE STRANGE OBJECT IN SKY
POP STAR MARRIES IN LONDON

2

Early this morning, a fire broke out in the big International Electronics factory near Bristol. The company makes robots and computers. The director of the company died in the fire. There was another fire in the same factory only two weeks ago. The police are investigating.

3

Yesterday evening, thousands of people saw a strange object in the sky. Some say it was round. Others say it was cigar-shaped. Later in the programme we talk to a schoolboy. He says he saw the object when it landed in a field near his home. He is sure it was a spaceship from another planet. He says he saw some people in the spaceship. What did they look like? Stay with us and find out.

4

And later in the programme we also talk to Judy Garrett. The famous pop star and dancer got married this morning in London. She is forty-three and her husband is twenty-one. They met in a restaurant only ten days ago. 'It was love at first sight,' Judy says. Find out more later in the programme.

Answer.

Picture one

1 What kind of programme do you think *The News in Focus* is?
2 What is going to happen in the programme?

Picture two

1 Where did the fire break out?
2 Something is very strange about this fire. What?
3 What happened to the director?

Picture three

1 What did people say about the object?
2 What does the schoolboy say about it?
3 What can you find out later in the programme?

Picture four

1 Who is Judy Garrett?
2 Talk about her and her husband.
3 Do you think there is anything strange about their marriage?
4 If you say 'Yes', say why you think this.

B

1 Stop and look.

How long ago did it happen?

The time is now six oh two (6.02) exactly. *The News in Focus* started exactly two minutes ago. When was that?

Let's say the date is Monday, the twenty-third (23rd). Judy met her husband ten days ago. When was that?
There was another fire at the International Electronics factory only two weeks ago. When was that?

MON	TUES	WED	THURS	FRI	SAT	SUN
2	3	4	5	6	7	8
9	10	11	12	13	14	15
16	17	18	19	20	21	22
23	24	25	26	27	28	29
30	31					

2 Ask and answer.

How long ago did you
- get up?
- have breakfast?
- come here?
- have your first English lesson?

3 Look at these old headlines.

All these things happened some time ago. What happened exactly?

Example: GANG STEALS MILLION DOLLARS FROM BANK
= A gang stole a million dollars from a bank.

1 **PICASSO DIES**

2 **WAR ENDS IN VIETNAM**

3 AMERICANS LAND ON MOON

4 **Famous film star marries policeman**

5 **Oil prices go up again**

6 POLICE ARREST KIDNAPPERS

4 Write and explain.

Think of some other things that happened some time ago. Write the headlines for them. Then say exactly what the headlines mean.

Unit One

C

1 Listen to this interview with Judy Garrett.

REPORTER: Tell us about your new husband, Judy. Where did you meet? And when?
JUDY: Here in London, in an Italian restaurant. It was only two weeks ago.
REPORTER: Tell us about it.
JUDY: Well, I don't know what to say, really. . . . I mean . . . when I first saw him, I knew that he was the man for me.
REPORTER: But how?
JUDY: Well . . . he . . . he was . . . very handsome. I mean, well . . . it wasn't just that, of course. He was tall . . . but not very tall. I don't like very tall men. But I don't like short men, either. And . . . there was something about his eyes . . . and his hair. It was dark and curly . . . I prefer men with dark, curly hair!
REPORTER: What happened then? After you first saw him, I mean.
JUDY: He spoke to me. That's when I really fell in love with him. When I heard his voice!
REPORTER: What did he say? Can you remember?
JUDY: Oh yes, I can remember exactly what he said! And I can remember exactly what I said, too!
REPORTER: What?
JUDY: 'Can I have your order, please?' 'Yes, I'd like some spaghetti, please.'
REPORTER: Pardon? You said . . . what?
JUDY: 'I'd like some spaghetti, please.' You see, I was in an Italian restaurant. And he was the waiter. I mean, I ordered some spaghetti from him. That's how it all began.

2 Ask and answer.

Ask other people in the class questions about the interview.

Where / How long ago | did ________?

Was he ________?

Did he have ________?

What did | he / she | do/say when ________?

3 Describe the kind of man Judy likes.

What about you? What kind of man or woman do you like?

4 This is part of a newspaper article. What are the missing words?

FILM STAR (1) SPAGHETTI AND (2) IN LOVE WITH WAITER.

Only two weeks (3) Judy Garrett (4) into an Italian restaurant in London and (5) some spaghetti. When the waiter (6) to her and she (7) his voice, she (8) in love with him.

1 What do they look like?

Which one (or ones) would you say:

a is middle aged?
b has got long, fair hair?
c has got a beard and a moustache?
d looks rather strange?
e is very tall?
f is rather fat?
g has got short, dark hair and a small moustache?
h is bald?
i is rather thin?
j has got a big scar on his forehead?
k has got big ears, too?
l has got dark skin and dark hair?

2 What do you think?

Do you think any of these people are:

a beautiful?
b handsome?
c attractive?
d rather ugly?

3 Speak and write.

Give a description of each person.

He / She | is about ________ years old.

He / She | has got ________ / is ________

Unit One

E

1 Listen to the interview.

A reporter interviews the schoolboy who saw the flying saucer. The schoolboy's name is Thomas Farley.

THOMAS: I was in that field over there. I often go there at night to look at the stars with my binoculars.

REPORTER: What exactly did the object look like?

THOMAS: Well, at first I thought it was long and thin, . . . like a cigar . . . but then I saw it was round and flat.

REPORTER: Round and flat. Like a saucer?

THOMAS: Yes, but with a big round ball in the middle.

REPORTER: How big was the object?

THOMAS: Oh . . . as big as a house. A small one.

REPORTER: You say you saw some people in the saucer.

THOMAS: Yes, I saw them when it landed. I was behind those trees, so they didn't see me.

REPORTER: What did they look like?

THOMAS: Well . . . one of them was a woman, I think. She had short, dark hair. And she was tall. Very tall.

REPORTER: And the other person?

THOMAS: He . . . it . . . had . . . you aren't going to believe this.

REPORTER: What? Go on.

THOMAS: His head was square.

REPORTER: Square? A square head?

THOMAS: Yes! With one big round eye in the middle and he had short legs . . . and four hands!

2 Answer.

1 Why was Thomas in the field?
2 Describe the object he saw.
3 Describe the people he saw.

3 Look and answer.

1 Look at the three objects in the picture (a, b and c). Describe them.
2 Two of them are different from the object Thomas saw. How?
3 Look at the person (d). How is he different from the second person Thomas saw?
4 Is anything the same? What?

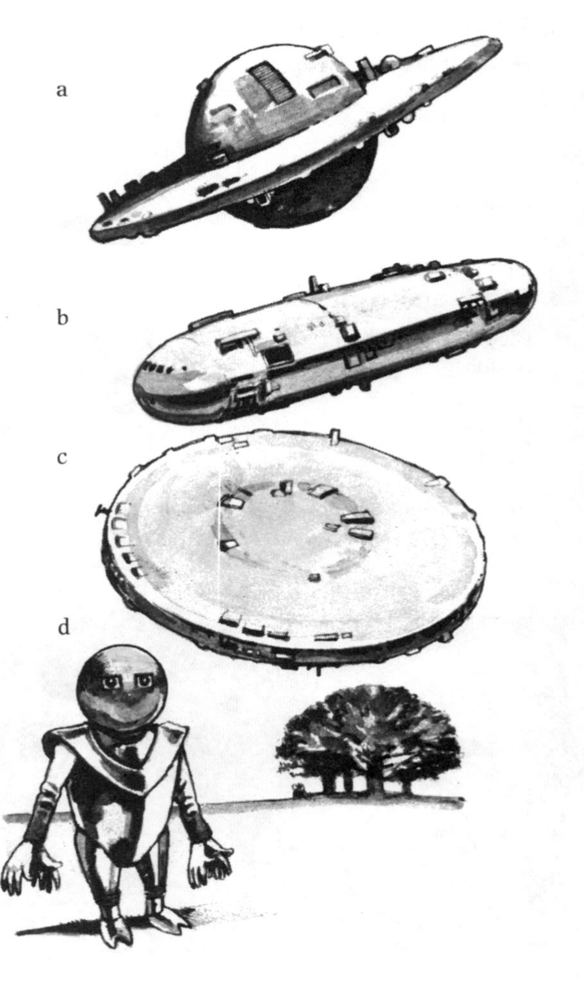

THE VISITOR

EPISODE ONE

This is a story in seventeen episodes. Read this episode. Then answer the questions.

1 Who is Tan-Lin?
2 What do you know about her planet?
3 Who is Mecco?
4 Describe him.

Tan-Lin was almost at the end of her long journey. She looked at her destination through the round window. It was a planet. In many ways the planet was like her own. It had two big oceans, rivers, continents and high mountains. But in other ways it was very different. This planet had only one moon. Her planet had two. And the people were different, too. She knew a lot about them and spoke three of their languages. They were dangerous people. They had wars. They killed.

'Are you ready, Tan-Lin?' Mecco asked.
'Yes, I'm ready,' she answered. Tan-Lin sat down in the big seat next to him. She put two big straps around her. One strap was around her legs. The other strap was around the top part of her body. Mecco pushed a button in front of him with one hand. With another hand he turned a small wheel. He pressed more buttons above him with his other two hands. They went down to the dark side of the planet.

When Thomas Farley first saw the light, he thought it was a star. He looked at the light through his binoculars.
'No, it can't be a star. It's moving,' he thought. The light came closer. Then he heard a strange noise. It was a low hum. The light stopped in the sky above him. Then it came down and landed in the field next to him. His mouth fell open. The low hum stopped. The strange object was dark in the light from the moon. Thomas heard another strange noise. A door opened.

Tan-Lin smelt the air of the planet for the first time. She walked through the door and stood on the ground. She looked up at the moon. She turned. Mecco was in the door.
'Goodbye, Mecco,' she said. The robot's one big eye was bright. He did not answer. He went back into the ship and the door closed. Tan-Lin walked to the road. The round object went up into the air. Then it was gone. Thomas watched with an open mouth. 'Nobody is going to believe me,' he thought.

Unit Two

A

This is part of another television programme. It is called *Theme of the Week*. Claire Walton does this programme, too.

In this week's programme our theme is *free time*. What do you do when you aren't working or at school? We asked a lot of people this question. Here are just a few of the answers.

My hobby is sky-diving. Do you know what that is? I jump from an aeroplane and fall through the air. I open my parachute only when I'm very close to the ground. Of course it's rather dangerous. Perhaps that's why I enjoy it. I think it's fun. Very few women do it. But we're just as good at it as men.

I'm very interested in music. In my free time I play and listen to it. I can play the guitar and the flute.
I enjoy all kinds of music but my favourite is folk music. Good folk music. I like classical music, too. But I prefer folk music. I'd like to have my own group some day.

My husband and I both work and we spend all our free time with our children. They're very important to us. We do a lot of things together. We go for picnics and long walks, and in the summer we all go on holiday together.

I love all kinds of sports but my favourite is tennis. But I don't enjoy watching it. I only enjoy playing it. And when I play I want to win! That's very important. I hate losing!

Unit Two

B

Answer.

What exactly was the question they asked a lot of people?

Picture one

1 Describe the first woman's hobby.
2 Why do you think it is dangerous?
3 Would you like to go skydiving? Why, or why not?

Picture two

1 Which instruments can the first man play?
2 What kinds of music does he like?
3 What kind does he prefer?
4 What about you? Do you like music? What kind do you prefer?

Picture three

1 What kinds of things does the second woman do in her free time?

Picture four

1 What about the second man?
2 What does he hate?
3 Which does he prefer: playing tennis or watching it?

1 Stop and look.

Here are some ways of finding out what other people do in their free time:

Are you interested in	music? sport? football?
What's your favourite	free time activity? sport? kind of music?
Do you enjoy	classical music? listening to folk music? tennis? playing tennis? watching it?

2 What about you?

Write about 100 words. Describe what you enjoy doing in your free time. Describe what you did in your free time yesterday.

3 What about other people?

Ask someone else in your class questions about what they enjoy doing in their free time. Also ask what they did yesterday or the day before in their free time.

4 Exercise.

Here are some things people enjoy doing in their free time. Say if you enjoy doing them or don't enjoy doing them.

Example: Some people eat in expensive restaurants.
= I enjoy eating in expensive restaurants.
Or I don't enjoy eating in expensive restaurants.

1 Some people watch football.
2 Some people play it.
3 Some people go to concerts.
4 Some people sit in pubs and drink a lot.
5 Some people lie in the sun.
6 Some people go for long walks.

Make two or more examples of things you enjoy or don't enjoy doing!

Unit Two

C

1 Listen to the dialogue.

Clive is a student at a Technical College in Brighton. Sheila works in the computer department of the college. It is evening and they are both going home.

CLIVE: Hi, Sheila. Are you going my way?
SHEILA: Yes, I am. Would you like a lift?
CLIVE: Oh, thanks a lot.
SHEILA: My car's over here. Get in.
(A few minutes later, in Sheila's car.)
CLIVE: Did you know that Judy Garrett is giving a concert here in Brighton?
SHEILA: When?
CLIVE: Friday evening. Would you like to go? I mean, I've got two tickets. Are you interested?
SHEILA: Yes, I am but . . .
CLIVE: Oh, good! Listen. Why don't we meet before the concert and . . .
SHEILA: Wait a moment Clive. You didn't let me finish. When is she giving the concert?
CLIVE: Friday evening. I told you.
SHEILA: Yes, but this Friday? Or next Friday?
CLIVE: This Friday. It starts at eight o'clock.
SHEILA: I'm sorry, Clive. I'd like to go very much but I can't. Not this Friday evening.
CLIVE: Why . . . why not?
SHEILA: I have to babysit.
CLIVE: Babysit?
SHEILA: Yes, for my sister. She's going out with her husband and I promised. I hope you understand. I mean, I'd prefer to go to the concert with you, but it just isn't possible.
CLIVE: Oh . . . I . . . I see. Some other time, perhaps.
SHEILA: Yes, Clive. Some other time. That would be very nice. Thank you all the same.

2 Answer.

1 What would Sheila like to do this Friday?
2 What is she going to do?
3 Why?

3 Role play 1.

Role A: You have two tickets for a concert or a football match. Ask B to go with you.

Role B: You would like to go but you have to study for an exam that evening or work late in your job.

4 Role play 2.

Take the same roles but this time there is no problem about going. But you have to discuss where and when to meet before.

1 Look and answer.

Here are a few things you can do this Saturday in London. What are they?
Which would you like to do?
You can do only one. Which would you prefer to do?

2 Questions.

1 Which one of the films is a very famous, romantic one?
2 Who is starring in it?
3 When can you see it on Saturday?
4 What can you say about the other one?
5 In one of the restaurants you can't eat meat. Which?
6 What do you get in the other one for £6.50?
7 In which restaurant can you hear a guitarist? When?
8 Here is part of a newspaper article about one of the matches. Which is it?

> The last time these two met, there were no goals. Let's hope the match this Saturday is more interesting.

3 Speak and write.

What are some of the things you enjoy doing at the weekend?
Talk about some of the things you don't enjoy doing.
What would you like to do this weekend?
Get answers to these questions from your neighbours, too.

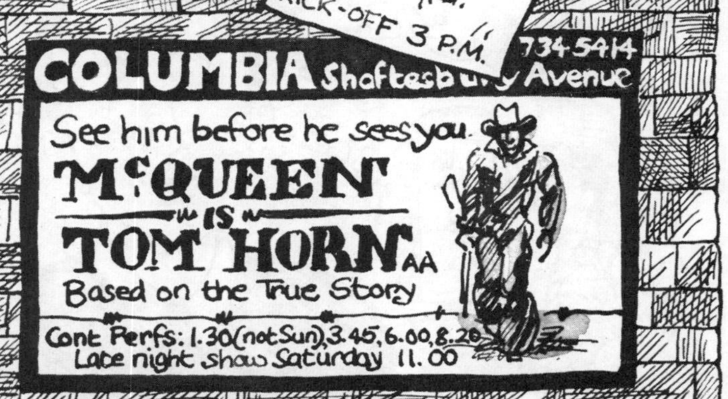

Unit Two

E

1 Stop and look.

To do (infinitive) or *doing* (gerund); that is the question!
With *want, hope, have, would like* and *would prefer* you always use the *to do* (infinitive) form.

I *want* We *hope* You *have* *Would* you *like* I'*d prefer*	*to*	*go* to the theatre tomorrow. *see* 'My Fair Lady' next week. *learn* some English now. *play* tennis this afternoon? *stay* in bed all day.

But with *like* (not *would like*) you can use *to do* or *doing*.

I *like*	*to watch* *watching* *to play* *playing*	football.

But if there is a verb after *enjoy*, it is always the *ing* form (gerund).

Clive doesn't *enjoy*	*going* to Technical College.
He *enjoys*	*playing* and *listening* to folk music.
I don't *enjoy*	*swimming* when the water is cold.
I *enjoy*	*living* in the sun.

2 Writing practice.

Use the *to do* or *doing* form of the verbs, like this:

Example: Clive would like (*go*) to the Judy Garrett concert.
= Clive would like to go to the Judy Garrett concert.

Example: He enjoys (*listen*) to her.
= He enjoys listening to her.

1 Clive enjoys (*go*) to concerts.

2 He would like (*go*) to the concert this Friday.

3 He hopes (*start*) his own folk music group.

4 He wants (*do*) this soon.

5 He can't do this now because he has (*go*) to Technical College.

6 He doesn't really enjoy (*study*) at the Technical College.

7 He would prefer (*study*) music at a college in London.

8 Clive likes (*play*) music and (*listen*) to it.

In one of these examples you can use both *to do* or the *doing* form. Which of the eight examples is this?

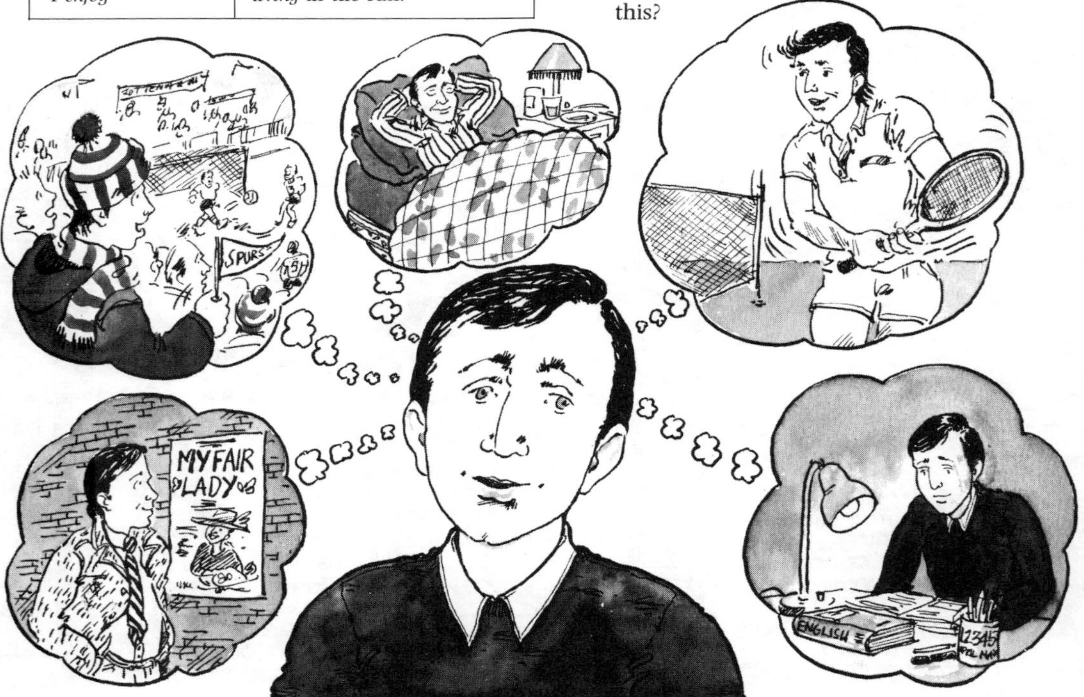

THE VISITOR

EPISODE TWO

The blue helicopter flew out to sea and turned west. After about twenty minutes the pilot pointed down to the sea below. The passenger was a middle-aged man. He wore a grey business suit. His hair and eyes were grey, too. He looked down. The yacht was there, as it always was. It was a large yacht, and like the helicopter, it was blue. The helicopter landed on the deck and the man in grey got out.

He went to a large cabin below the deck. A younger man with cold, blue eyes sat behind a large desk.
'Good morning, Mr Shandor,' the man in grey said. He smiled.
'Good morning, Harlan. Sit down,' the man with cold blue eyes answered. He didn't smile. The man in grey sat down and took some papers out of a grey leather briefcase. He handed them to the younger man.
'Here are the plans for the new robot,' he said. The man with cold blue eyes studied the plans for about five minutes.
'Yes, they're all right. You can go ahead with them, Harlan,' he said.

Harlan took some newspapers out of the briefcase, too. He pointed to a headline on the front page of one of them.
'COMPANY DIRECTOR DIES IN FACTORY FIRE' the headline said. Harlan smiled.
'The police think it was an accident, Mr Shandor. Here. You can read the article.'
Shandor read the article. For the first time, he smiled, too. But it was a cold smile, like his blue eyes.
'Very good, Harlan. But I see that the police are investigating the fire.'
'Yes, Mr Shandor. But what can they find out? Nothing!'
'Not if you followed my orders,' Shandor said.
'Oh, I did, Mr Shandor. I did!'

Shandor looked at his watch.
'And now what about the other business. Yesterday you told me about one of the engineers at our Southampton factory. You say he's giving information to a journalist. Is that right?' he asked.
'Yes, exactly. And we listened to all his phone calls yesterday evening. The journalist phoned him at home. They're going to meet this evening in Southampton, Mr Shandor!'
Shandor thought for a moment. Then he looked at the third man in the cabin. The third man sat in front of the door. He never moved. His eyes were open but he never blinked. He wore strange, round glasses. Shandor smiled once again.
'I think this is a job for one of our friends here,' he said.
Harlan looked at the third man and smiled, too.

Questions.

1 Why do you think Shandor and Harlan are interested in the factory fire?
2 What do they say about a journalist and an engineer?

Unit Three

A

Time for Claire Walton with *The News in Focus.*

Good evening. In *The News in Focus* this evening we're again going to look at the stories behind these headlines.

MOTHER OF THREE WINS £750,000
GORILLAS LEARN TO DRIVE
BIG DIAMOND ROBBERY IN CENTRE OF LONDON

1

Life has not been easy for Mrs Watson. Her husband died five years ago and left her with three children and no money. She found it difficult to get a job. She was very poor. But Mrs Watson is richer today. Much richer. The attractive young widow won £750,000 in the Football Pools yesterday evening. She talks to us later in the programme. She doesn't know exactly what she is going to do with all the money. But one thing is clear. Life is going to be easier and better for her from now on!

2

This is something you don't see very often – a gorilla driving a car. But perhaps you're going to see this more often from now on. In a school in Boston, in the United States, gorillas and chimpanzees are learning to do this and other things. Their teachers say that some of the gorillas are better drivers than most people. 'Gorillas are really very intelligent. Chimpanzees are even more intelligent. But they're too small to drive a car,' one teacher said today.

3

This afternoon a man and a woman walked into an expensive shop in London and asked to see some gold watches. The salesman went to the manager's office to get some. They followed him. Then they took out guns and told the manager to open the safe. Two diamonds were in the safe. The smaller one cost £200,000. The bigger one cost £300,000! The couple took the diamonds and left the watches.

Answer.

What is a 'mother of three'?
How do you think she won the money?
Explain the other two headlines.

Picture one

1 What happened to Mrs Watson five years ago?
2 Why wasn't life easy for her?
3 Why is life going to be 'easier and better for her from now on'?

Picture two

1 What don't you see very often?
2 What is happening in a school in Boston?
3 What do the teachers say about gorillas and chimpanzees?

Picture three

1 What do you think the man and woman said when they walked into the shop?
2 What do you think they said in the manager's office?
3 What happened then?

1 Stop and look.

bigger/better cheaper/more expensive younger/more attractive	than

Ponzo	*Donald*
Age: 9	Age: 24
Height: 135 cm	Height: 180 cm
IQ: ?	IQ: 130

Which of these two is:

a older?
b taller?
c more intelligent?

Who do you think is:

a stronger?
b more attractive?
c a better driver?

2 Look and answer.

1 Which watch is bigger – watch (a) or watch (b)?

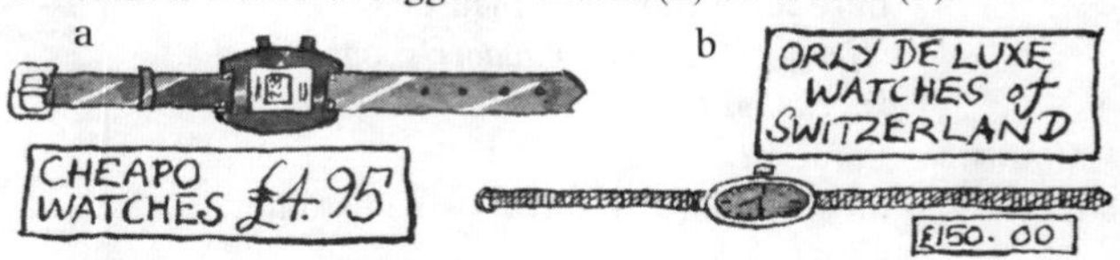

2 Which one is smaller?
3 Which one is more expensive?
4 Which do you think is better – the more expensive or the cheaper one?

3 Finish the sentences.

1 (*tall*) Donald is ________ than Ponzo.
2 (*intelligent*) He is probably ________ ________ ________ Ponzo, too.
3 (*cheap*) This watch is too expensive. Have you got a ________ one?
4 (*expensive*) Why is this watch ________ ________ than that one?
5 (*good*) Do you really think that this watch is ________ ________ that one?

Unit Three

C

1 Listen to the dialogue.

This was the conversation in the expensive shop in London. A man and a woman walked in and . . .

SALESMAN:	Can I help you?
WOMAN:	Yes, we're looking for a watch. It's for me.
SALESMAN:	I see. What price are you interested in?
MAN:	The price doesn't matter. But it must be a gold watch.
WOMAN:	And automatic. I must have an automatic watch!
SALESMAN:	Hmm . . . something like this, perhaps. It's one of our best watches. Made in Switzerland. Fully automatic. With a calendar and . . .
MAN:	It's nice . . . but haven't you got anything better?
SALESMAN:	Better? Better than this? Well, we have some *Orly de luxe* watches . . . probably the best watch in the world. But I'm afraid they're far more expensive than this one. They cost . . .
MAN:	Would you show us one, please?
WOMAN:	Yes, could we see one of them, please?
SALESMAN:	They're in the manager's office. You see, we don't . . .
MAN:	Could you possibly get one or two of them now?
SALESMAN:	Er . . . yes, of course. Would you wait here for a moment, please? (*He goes to the manager's office and knocks on the door.*)
MANAGER:	Come in.
SALESMAN:	Mr Crawford, I have two customers who . . .
WOMAN:	All right! Hands up! Stand over there!
MANAGER/ SALESMAN:	What in the world . . .
MAN:	Shut up! And open that safe! Come on! Open it!
MANAGER:	I . . . I can't open it.
MAN:	What do you mean? You *must* open it.
MANAGER:	You told me to put my hands up. How can I open the safe with my hands up?

2 Answer.

1 What did the man and woman ask to see?
2 What did they really want?
3 Explain how they got into the manager's office.
4 Describe what happened then.

3 Role play.

Role A: You are in a shop. You are looking for a good watch. It must be fully automatic, tell the day and the date and be waterproof. You don't want to spend more than £50.

Role B: You work in the shop. Try to sell A the *True Time* electronic watch. You think it is far better than cheaper watches. It costs £60.

1 Stop and look.

Asking people to do things.

> Would you wait a moment please?
> Could you show me some watches?
> Can you tell me the time, please?

Would is very polite. So is *could*. People often use *could* and *can* when they aren't sure if the other person can do it.

Telling people to do things.

> Open that safe!
> You must open it!
> Put your hands up!
> Stop that! You must stop it!

This isn't very polite. But you can make it more polite with the word *please*: *Come in, please.*

2 What are they saying in the three situations?

A: ________ you open the door for me, ________?
B: Of ________.

A: ________ your food!
B: But I don't ________ it!
A: I don't care. You ________ eat it!

A: Excuse me. ________ you tell me the way to Oxford Street, ________ ?
B: I'm ________, but I ________. I'm a stranger here, too.

3 Buying a radio.

What are the missing words in the dialogue?

SALESMAN: ___(1)___ I help you?
CUSTOMER: Yes, I'm ___(2)___ for a radio.
SALESMAN: How ___(3)___ did you want to pay?
CUSTOMER: Oh, ___(4)___ £30 and £40.
SALESMAN: Something ___(5)___ this?
CUSTOMER: Hmm. It's too big.
Have you got something ___(6)___ ?
SALESMAN: There's this ___(7)___. It's very small.
CUSTOMER: And how much does it ___(8)___ ?
SALESMAN: £45.
CUSTOMER: That's ___(9)___ than I want to pay.
Have you got anything ___(10)___ ?

Here are the missing words. Where do they belong?

a) much b) more c) Can d) between
e) smaller f) like g) cost h) cheaper
i) looking j) one

4 Now listen to the dialogue on tape.

Unit Three

E

1 What is wrong here?

Read the two newspaper articles. Sometimes whole lines from one article are mixed up with the other article. (This sometimes happens, even in the best English newspapers.) Which lines from the first article do you think belong in the second article? Can you find lines in the second article that belong in the first one?

NEWS AN

FRIDAY OCTOBER 23 1981

Chimps learn to talk

At a school in Boston, three
chimpanzees are learning how to
speak English. One of the three
chimps is called Suzie and she
5 already has a small but useful
vocabulary. She can now say
£750,000. She told our reporter
'One of the other drivers showed
me how to do the Pools one day.
10 But this isn't the same as real
language because Suzie can't use
these words in different ways for
different situations. For example,
she can't use them in questions like
15 'What are you going to do with all
that money? I don't know the
words, Suzie knows some phrases but
not the grammar. Without grammar,
words are just words and not a real
20 language.

Van driver wins £750,000

Three years ago, Mrs Susan Watson
learned how to drive. This was a
very important step in her life
because six months ago she got a
5 job driving a van. In a strange
way this job helped her to win
things like 'banana', 'good' and
whole phrases like 'My name is
Suzie' and 'I want more water'.
10 At first I wasn't very interested
but then I started doing them all
the time. Then I won all this money.
It's wonderful. A lot of people
always ask me the same question.
15 'Do you want a banana?' and
'What's your name?' In other
answer, but I think I'd like to buy
a much bigger house and go on a nice
holiday with all my children.'

2 Now answer these questions.

1 What did the van driver win?
2 Why was it an important step in her life when she learned how to drive?
3 What is the question people always ask her?
4 What is her answer?
5 Who is Suzie?
6 What is she learning to do?
7 What are some of the things she can say?
8 Why isn't this 'real language'?

THE VISITOR

EPISODE THREE

Tony Redford was a journalist. He wrote articles for a magazine called *Business News*. He was a young man, of medium height. He had rather long, dark brown hair and a small moustache. There was always a very serious look on his face. He looked even more serious that morning. He was in his boss's office. His boss was called Liz Davis and she was the editor of *Business News*. She was short and had red hair. As usual, she had a cigarette in her hand. She blew a cloud of smoke at him.

'Well, Tony. Your first article about the electronics industry is going to the printer's this afternoon. It's very interesting. But what about your second article? Are you sure you can write two articles about the electronics industry? I mean, isn't one enough?' she asked.
'Listen, Liz, I tell you that the second article is going to be more interesting than the first! Far more interesting!'

Liz looked at him and puffed again on her cigarette.
'Why do you think so?' she asked.
'I'm going to get some information this evening about a small company called Shandor Electronics. The director is probably one of the best electronics engineers in the world. But nobody knows very much about him. Not even where he comes from. He lives on a yacht. He never visits his factory in Southampton. Someone goes to the yacht from the factory every morning in a helicopter. Now . . . I know an engineer who works at that factory. His name is Presley, and Presley tells me that Shandor has plans for a new kind of electronic brain. It's much smaller but far better than other electronic brains on the market today. I'm going to meet Presley in Southampton this evening. I'm going to use the information I get from him in my second article. Presley says Shandor is going to make some new kind of robot, too. But he doesn't know very much about that. It's one of the company's biggest secrets!'

Liz Davis puffed on her cigarette. She looked more interested than before.
'All right, Tony. Go ahead with your second article. But finish it no later than the end of next week! Do you understand? I must have it at the end of next week! No later than that!'

In a street not far away from the offices of *Business News*, a tall young woman stopped in front of a newspaper stand. She was very polite when she spoke to the newspaper seller. Her English was very careful and very correct. The seller thought she was probably a foreign visitor. The tall young woman stared at one of the headlines in the paper.
'COMPANY DIRECTOR DIES IN FACTORY FIRE' the headline said.

Questions.

1 Why is Tony Redford so interested in Shandor?
2 Who is Redford going to meet?

Unit Four

A

This is part of another *Theme of the Week* programme. It is about *work*.

1 Look at the pictures.

In this evening's programme, we asked six people about the jobs they do. Perhaps you can get an idea of their jobs from these pictures.

2 Answer.

1 Which one of these people do you think is
   a an assembly-line worker?
   b a diver?
   c a stewardess?
2 What are the other jobs?
3 Which one do you think is
   a dangerous?
   b boring?
   c dirty?
4 Who do you think says these things?
   a You're still very ill, but you're getting better.
   b Excuse me, but I don't think your seat belt is fastened.
   c I really get bored doing exactly the same thing day after day!
5 Which of these jobs would you like to do? Which wouldn't you like to do? Why?

1

2

3

4

5

6

1 And this is what the people said about their jobs. Can you guess who said what?

It's an interesting job. I meet a lot of interesting people. Some of them give me big tips. Some of them are drunk and don't know what they're doing. On some days I earn a lot. On others I earn very little. A lot depends on the weather.

It's a very hard job, really. Very long hours. I often work at night. There are a lot of bad accidents at night, you know. I'm married but I don't see my husband very often. He's a teacher and is in school all day. And I'm often in the hospital all night. I'm usually very tired when I see him in the morning.

Of course the pay is good. But it's hard. And very dangerous. Not long ago, for example, a big fish swam past me. It was a shark. Thank God it wasn't hungry. It wasn't very interested in me.

It isn't a bad job, really. I've always been interested in cars. Even when I was a little girl. I really enjoy working on them. What I don't like is all the grease and dirt. It's really hard to get it all off. Perhaps that's why some people think it's a strange job for a woman. But I don't.

In some ways I'm just like a waitress, but I don't get any tips. Of course, I travel a lot. New York, Hong Kong, Athens. But I never stay in those places very long. I've been with the airline for six years now. I think I'd like to do something different. I mean, do another job.

Me? Well . . . I've had this job for ten years now. It's safe. It's clean. It's easy. In many ways the working conditions are very good. But it's boring! Always the same, day after day. And the pay is very poor. That's why I work a lot of overtime. Forty hours a week and then an extra eight hours overtime, almost every week!

2 Here are some of the questions the interviewer asked the six people. Who were the questions for? What were the answers?

1 What kind of fish was it?
2 What are some of the cities you go to?
3 How much overtime do you work?
4 Why don't you see him very often?
5 What does your husband do?
6 Do you earn the same every day?
7 Why do they think it's a strange job for you to do?
8 What about tips?
9 Why do you say it's boring?
10 Why do you work at nights?

3 Here are two new kinds of question. Look at them. Who answered them? What were the answers?

How long *have you been* with the airline?
How long *have you had* this job?

Unit Four

C

1 Stop and look.

This man started in this office 30 years ago. He was a clerk then.

He is a clerk now. He *has been* a clerk for 30 years. He *has had* the same job all that time.

'*I've been* a clerk for 30 years now. *I've had* the same job for 30 years.'

2 Remember.

He She	*has*	*been* with this company *had* this job	for	30 years. six months. a long time. only a short time.
I/You We/They	*have*			

Write:	*Say:*	*Notice again!*
he has been	He's been	We use this form to talk about something that began in the past but comes into the present.
I have been	I've been	
We have been	We've been	

3 Talk and write about Clive Peters.

has *had* *been*

1 Clive ________ been a student for three years.
2 He lives in Brighton. He has ________ there for three years, too.
3 He ________ got a small car.
4 He has ________ it for about a year now.

4 What is Clive saying?

1 I ________ a student here at Brighton Technical College for three years.
2 I live in Brighton now. I ________ here for three years.
3 I ________ car. I ________ it for about a year now.
4 ________ you ________ a car? How long ________ you ________ it?

5 Ask and answer other people.

How long have you been | here? / in ________? / a student/teacher/mechanic/clerk? etc.

How long have you had | a car? / a bike? / that watch? / your job? etc.

1 The wrong sex or the wrong clothes? Listen to the dialogue.

Sylvia and Larry both work for a big company in London. They work in different departments. They are having lunch in the canteen.

SYLVIA: We've got a new manager in our department.
LARRY: Oh? You hoped to get that job, didn't you?
SYLVIA: Yes, I did.
LARRY: I'm sorry. That's too bad. Who is it? Who got the job, I mean?
SYLVIA: Someone called Drexler. Carl Drexler. He's been with the company only two years. I've been here longer. And I know more about the job, too!
LARRY: Hmm. Why do you think they gave it to him and not to you?
SYLVIA: Because I'm the wrong sex, of course!
LARRY: You mean you didn't get the job because you're a woman?
SYLVIA: Yes, that was probably it! It isn't fair.
LARRY: What sort of clothes does he wear?
SYLVIA: A dark suit. White shirt. A tie. Why?
LARRY: Perhaps that had something to do with it.
SYLVIA: You mean you think I didn't get the job because I come to work in jeans and a sweater?
LARRY: It's possible, isn't it?
SYLVIA: Do you really think I should wear different clothes?
LARRY: Well . . . perhaps you should think about it.
SYLVIA: Why should I wear a skirt? Or a dress?
LARRY: I'm not saying you should. I'm saying you should think about it. That's all!
SYLVIA: Why should I do that? I'm good at my job! That's the only important thing!
LARRY: Hmm. Perhaps it should be the only important thing. But it isn't. Not in this company.

2 Answer.

1 What was the job that Sylvia wanted?
2 Why does she think she didn't get it?
3 What does Larry think?
4 He tells her that perhaps she *should* do something. What?

3 Role play.

Role A: You work for a big company. You always wear jeans and a sweater. Other people get better jobs in the company. You don't. Go to your boss and find out why.

Role B: You are A's boss. You like A's work. But you think A's clothes are wrong for the job. The company is rather conservative about these things. Suggest that A should get some different clothes.

Use language like:
I think you should ________.
Don't you think you should ________?

Unit Four

E

1 Stop and look.

Perhaps you *should wear* a suit to work. Do you think I *should buy* some new clothes? The company *shouldn't give* him the job. He/she *shouldn't get* the job.
Should I *wear* different clothes? What *should* Ted *do*? *Should* we *do* this? Why *should* I *do* it?

2 Who do you think should get the job?

A big company has four jobs open. Look at the pictures opposite and say who should get each job. Think quickly! Decide fast!

JOB 1: EXPORT MANAGER
sees a lot of important customers; eats in expensive restaurants

JOB 2: OFFICE HELPER
makes the tea; keeps things clean; runs around a lot

JOB 3: DELIVERY VAN DRIVER
drives a van; lifts things; gets dirty

JOB 4: PERSONNEL MANAGER
hires and fires people; should have a lot of experience with men and women

3 Discuss with others in the class.

Do you think ________ should be the ________?
Should ________ get the job of ________?
Who should get Job 1, 2, etc.?

4 Write these sentences – finish them with *should* or *shouldn't*.

1 I don't think children ________ smoke.
2 The doctor told me I ________ drink so much coffee.
3 When ________ I phone you tomorrow?
4 There are two good films on. Which one ________ we see?
5 Kate often hits her husband. She ________ do that.
6 If you want to get a job, you ________ wear those dirty jeans!

WHAT PEOPLE SAY

Now turn to page 103 and listen to the tape to find out what people say about their jobs.

THE VISITOR

EPISODE FOUR

Questions.

Read this episode with these questions in mind. Answer them after you read the episode.

1 What do you learn about the man called Presley?
2 What happens to him in the episode?
3 Why do you think it happens to him?

John Presley wasn't very happy with his job. He was a computer engineer with Shandor Electronics. He worked in their Southampton factory. In some ways, it was more like a prison than a factory. There was a high fence around it. Men with dogs walked along it, day and night.
'I've been with the company for more than three years but they don't tell me very much. There are all sorts of things they don't want me to know,' he often told his wife. But Presley was a very intelligent man. He found out a lot of things the company didn't want him or other people to know. He knew a journalist who worked for a magazine in London. His name was Tony Redford. Redford was very interested in Presley's information.

Presley came home from work and cooked dinner for himself and his wife. She was the manageress of a supermarket and worked long hours.
'I have to go out again this evening,' he told her when she came home.
'Why?'
'I'm helping a journalist write an article about the electronics industry. I think I can earn some money that way,' he told her.

Presley lived in a small village in a forest near Southampton. He backed his car out of the garage. His wife waved to him.
'Be careful. Don't drink too much,' she said. He laughed and drove away.

He didn't notice the light blue car and the dark green van. They were parked near his house. When he left, they followed him. He had to go to Southampton to meet Redford. There was very little traffic on the road. The van and the car stayed behind him. Suddenly the van overtook him. The light blue car was close behind Presley. He noticed its lights in the rear view mirror He wanted to go faster, but the van in front stopped him. He tried to overtake the van but it went faster, too. Suddenly Presley felt a bump. It was the car behind. It bumped into him again and pushed him towards the van. He was like a small piece of iron in a magnet! He turned and twisted on his driving wheel but nothing happened! He felt he no longer had control of his car.

The van and the car began to go very fast, and he was between them. He screamed. They came to a bridge over a river. Suddenly the van in front broke free. The car behind drove faster and pushed Presley towards the side of the bridge. He shot through it like a bullet. Presley screamed again. He and his car dropped down into the dark water far below the bridge. The car sank like a stone.

The van and the car didn't stop. They turned into a side road before they got to Southampton. Nobody saw them. The next morning the police found Presley and his car in the river. The newspapers said it was a very strange accident.

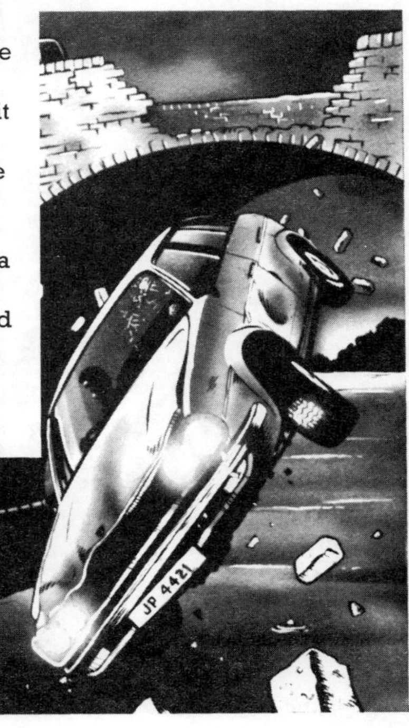

Unit Five

A

For our first story this evening in ***The News in Focus*** **we look at a new kind of contest. It's called *Personality of the Year*. To win it, you have to be attractive. And you have to be intelligent, too.**

Ask and answer.

How	old / tall / heavy	is ________? Do you think ______ is very handsome?

Who is the	oldest? / youngest? / tallest?	Who do you think is the most	beautiful? / handsome?

1 And here are the interviews with three of the contestants.

Interview 1.

CLAIRE: Tell me about yourself, Bruce.
BRUCE: Well . . . uh . . . what do you want to know?
CLAIRE: Well . . . what do you do? What's your job?
BRUCE: Uh . . . I . . . I work for my father . . .
CLAIRE: And what does your father do?
BRUCE: He . . . uh . . . owns a factory.
CLAIRE: What are you interested in?
BRUCE: What?
CLAIRE: What are you interested in?
BRUCE: Oh. Hmm . . . uh . . . football . . . yes . . . football. . . .
CLAIRE: Anything else?
BRUCE: Well . . . uh . . . women. Oh, and I like to fight – box, I mean. I'm very interested in boxing.

Interview 2.

CLAIRE: What do you do for a living, Jenny?
JENNY: I work in a department store. In the cosmetics department.
CLAIRE: And your main interests?
JENNY: I'm very old-fashioned.
CLAIRE: Could you explain that?
JENNY: I'm interested in things like cooking. And gardening. Some people think women . . . modern women shouldn't be interested in those things. But I am.
CLAIRE: What are your ambitions in life?
JENNY: Old-fashioned ones.
CLAIRE: What do you mean?
JENNY: I'd like to get married. And have children. I'm very interested in children. I think I'd like a very big family.

Interview 3.

CLAIRE: What do you do, Sue?
SUE: I'm a computer programmer, I work for one of the biggest computer companies in the world. I've been with them for two years. It's a very interesting job.
CLAIRE: What are your main interests?
SUE: It's difficult to tell you all of them. I'm very interested in mathematics – it was my best subject at school – and also in philosophy, foreign languages – I speak three of them – classical music, chess, yoga and gymnastics.
CLAIRE: Gymnastics?
SUE: Yes. I think everyone should do something active. We all need exercise. I do gymnastics . . . I also jog, and then I often . . .
CLAIRE: Thank you very much, Sue . . . I'm afraid that's all we have time for.

2 Ask and answer.

What does ________ do?

What is | he / she | interested in?

3 Speak and write.

Bruce	works in/for ________
Sue	likes/is interested in ________
Jenny	would like to ________ (etc.)

4 What do you think?

Is ________ *more* | *interesting* / *intelligent* | than ________?

Who do you think is the *most* | *interesting?* / *intelligent?*

Unit Five

C

1 Look and read.

In this evening's programme, we also have a look at prices. Different prices for exactly the same thing. We looked at three different things. And we went to three different places. We compared the price of each thing. The result was surprising. This is what we found.

2 Ask and answer.

1 How much does the ________ cost at ________?
2 Where is it the cheapest?
3 Where is it the most expensive?
4 Which is the best place to buy the ________?

3 Speak and write.

You can say and write this about the cassette player:

I compared the price of the cassette player at three places. It was cheapest at Discount 85 and most expensive at Sellbury's. In other words, the best place to buy the cassette is at Discount 85.

Now speak and write about the other two things.

Unit Five

D

1 Here are three dialogues in a department store. Which dialogue goes with which picture?

Dialogue 1.

MAN: I'm not satisfied with it.
SALESWOMAN: Why not? What's wrong with it?
MAN: Sometimes it goes fast. And sometimes it goes slow. And the alarm doesn't work, either.
SALESWOMAN: Would you like another one?
MAN: No. Can I have my money back?
SALESWOMAN: Hmm . . . have you got a receipt?
MAN: A receipt?
SALESWOMAN: Yes. I must see your receipt. You can't have your money back without a receipt.
MAN: Oh, I'm not certain, but I think I've lost it.

Dialogue 2.

WOMAN: Which of the two do you think is better? I mean, what's the difference between them?
SALESMAN: Well . . . this one costs more, but it has a much better sound. This part of it is made of wood, not plastic. And there's a tone control, too.
WOMAN: I only want it for the kitchen. I like to listen to the news at breakfast time.
SALESMAN: Hmm . . . well, the other one is good for the money. It's much cheaper. We sell a lot of them and all our customers are satisfied with them.
WOMAN: Hmm . . . I'd like the cheaper one, please. Can I pay by cheque?
SALESMAN: Certainly.

Dialogue 3.

MAN: Can you deliver it, please?
SALESWOMAN: It depends where you live, sir.
MAN: In Camden Town.
SALESWOMAN: Yes, we deliver there. But it costs two pounds fifty.
MAN: All right. But I'm only in on Saturday.
SALESWOMAN: Morning or afternoon?
MAN: Afternoon, please, if that's possible.

2 Answer.

1 What is the man in the first dialogue talking about?
2 What does he want?
3 Why?
4 Do you think he is going to get it?
5 Why (Or why not?)

6 What does the woman want?
7 Why is one better than the other?
8 Which one does she buy?
9 Why?
10 How does she pay for it?

11 What did the man buy?
12 Is he going to take it home with him?

a

b

c

Unit Five

E

1 Stop and look.

This happens with adjectives of one or two syllables (e.g. *high*, *happy*).
Give more examples with *tall*, *short*, *dirty*.

But notice what happens with *good* and *bad*.

Do you remember the three interviews in section B?

Use *more* ________ and the *most* ________ with adjectives of more than two syllables:
in-ter-est-ing/beau-ti-ful/terr-i-ble

2 In this exercise make your own examples with the words shown.

1 (*high*) Is Ben Nevis ________ than Mt Everest?

2 What is the ________ mountain in the world?

3 (*young*) Billy is five and Mary is four. Which one is ________?

4 (*young*) Tom Edwards is only 16 and he is a pilot. He is one of the ________ pilots in the world.

5 (*dirty*) My job is very ________. It is one of the ________ jobs in the world.

6 (*good*) This summer is ________ but I think last summer was ________.

7 (*good*) What is the ________ summer you can remember?

8 (*bad*) And what was the ________ summer you can remember?

9 (*bad*) Was 1979 really ________ than 1978?

10 (*good*) I hope next summer is ________ than this one.

11 (*terrible*) That was one of the ________ days of my life.

12 (*boring*) My job is ________ than yours.

13 (*dangerous*) I have one of the ________ jobs in the world.

14 (*expensive*) Diamonds are ________ than books.

THE VISITOR

EPISODE FIVE

Tony Redford is a journalist. He wants to find out more about a strange engineer, Thomas Shandor. A man called Harlan visits Shandor every day in his yacht.

Harlan showed Shandor Tony Redford's article about the electronics industry.
'As you can see, there's very little about you or our company in the magazine,' he said with a nervous smile.
Shandor looked at him with his cold, blue eyes.
'Perhaps Redford knows more about us than is in this article. Do you really know how much Presley told him?' Harlan's smile became more nervous.
'I don't think Presley told him very much. He only saw Redford . . .' Shandor stopped him.
'I want you to find out exactly how much Redford knows! It's another job for one of our friends here,' he said. He and Harlan looked at the third man in the cabin. As usual, he sat near the door and never moved. He was a very big man. He wore strange, round glasses.

That afternoon, Tony Redford sat in the office of his boss, Liz Davis.
'Presley was on his way to see me when the accident happened. That is, if it was an accident,' he told her.
'What do you mean? Do you think it wasn't an accident?' she asked.
'I don't know. Presley was a very careful driver. How could he lose control of his car like that?'
'But if someone killed him, who was it, Tony? And why? Why, Tony? Why?' Tony didn't answer the question.

A few hours later, the telephone rang in Tony's office.
'I'd like to speak to Mr Tony Redford, please.' It was a woman's voice. She spoke slow, careful, but very correct English. Tony thought he noticed an accent, but it wasn't strong.
'Speaking,' he said.
'Mr Redford, I read your article about the electronics industry. I'd like to ask you a few questions about it.'
Tony looked at his watch. He had a lot of work to do and had very little time for conversations like this.
'Well, I'm afraid I'm very busy at the moment. But if you write a letter . . .'
'No, Mr Redford. I must see you! In your article you wrote about a man called Shandor. I must find out more about him!'
Suddenly Tony was more interested.
'Why? Who are you? And what do you know about Shandor?' he asked.
'Please meet me tomorrow evening at nine o'clock. I know you often go to a pub called *The Brunswick*. Be there, please! It's very important!'
'Just a moment. Who are you? What's your name?' Tony asked. But there was no answer. The woman hung up.

Questions.

1 What do you think Tony is going to do?
2 What do you think he should do?
3 Why?

Unit Six

A

The theme of this week's programme is: *Where do you live and what do you think of it?* Let's begin by comparing four different places.

London is one of the biggest cities in the world. It has a population of over 8 million. Some people like it very much because there is a lot to do there and it is very interesting. There are hundreds of cinemas, theatres, museums and restaurants there. But other people don't like it because there is so much traffic and noise everywhere.

Brighton is a medium-sized town with a population of around 300,000. It is on the coast, about 50 miles from London. Of course it isn't as interesting as London. But the air is a lot cleaner and better. There are a few factories there, but not many. It isn't very easy to find a good job there. But there are a lot of hotels and language schools in the town. In the summer the town is full of tourists.

Stockport is about as big as Brighton. It is in the north of England, near Manchester. In fact, it is almost a suburb of Manchester now. Stockport isn't a very clean town. There is a lot of industry there. That is why the air is rather dirty. But the people are very friendly.

Killbrae is a very small village. Exactly 213 people live there. It is in the north of Scotland. It is a very beautiful place and the air is very clean. But there are very few jobs in Killbrae. There is no industry there. There is very little to do. There aren't any cinemas or things like that in the village. And the people aren't very friendly.

Answer.

What is this week's programme about? How is Claire going to begin the programme?

Look at the answers. What are the questions?

Picture one
1 Over 8 million.
2 Because there's a lot to do there.
3 Because it's very noisy.

Picture two
1 No, it's much smaller.
2 Yes, but only a few.
3 No, it isn't.
4 Yes, but mostly in the summer.

Picture three
1 It's in the north, near Manchester.
2 No, it isn't.
3 Because there's a lot of industry there.
4 Yes, they are.

Picture four
1 In the north of Scotland.
2 Exactly 213.
3 Yes, it is.
4 No, there isn't.
5 Because there's no industry there.
6 They aren't very friendly.

B

1 Stop and look.

How *much*	industry work	is there in Killbrae? – Very little.
How *many*	factories jobs	are there? – Very few.

Finish these questions and answers:
1 How ________ big towns ________ there in the north of Scotland?
Very ________.
2 How ________ money can you earn in Killbrae?
Very ________.
3 How ________ tourists visit Stockport every year?
Very ________.
4 How ________ factories are there in Brighton?
Very ________.
5 How ________ food can you buy today for £1?
Oh, very ________.

2 Answer.

Brighton is smaller *than* London.
Stockport is *as* big *as* Brighton.

Use *as* or *than*:
1 Brighton is much bigger ________ Killbrae.
2 Killbrae is smaller ________ Stockport.
3 But the people in Killbrae aren't ________ friendly ________ the people in Stockport.
4 Do you think English food is ________ good ________ French food?
5 Is London bigger ________ Paris?
6 Do you think it is ________ interesting ________ New York?

3 What about where you live?

Write a short description (100–150 words) of the place where you live. Answer these questions about it:
1 Where is it exactly?
2 What is the population?
3 Is there any industry there? If so, what?
4 What is there to do there?
5 Is it dirty, beautiful, ugly or clean?
What else can you write about it?

Unit Six

C

1 Find the dialogue.

Claire interviews an old man who lives in Killbrae. His name is Gavin Cass. Claire's questions are on the left. Find Gavin's answers to the questions on the right.

1 Where were you born, Gavin?
2 When did you come to Killbrae?
3 And why did you come?
4 So how long have you been living here now?
5 What do you think of it?
6 What are the people like?
7 You mean, they don't like strangers?
8 Would you like to live somewhere else?

a Because my wife got a job here as a schoolteacher.
b They're not very friendly.
c No, I wouldn't. Not really.
d In Inverness, about 50 miles away.
e No, they don't. And they think I'm one because I wasn't born here.
f A long time ago, when I was a young man.
g The village? Oh, I think it's very beautiful.
h For 50 years now.

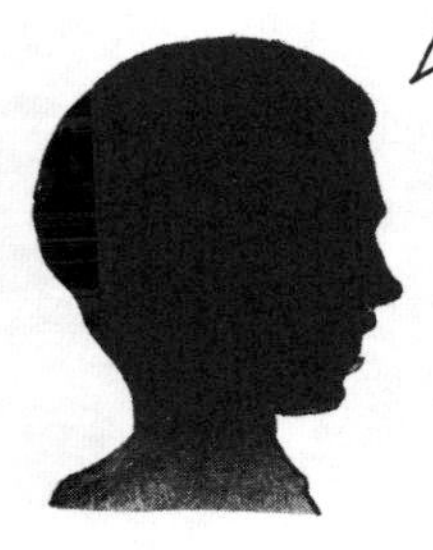

2 You can listen to the complete dialogue on tape.

3 Listen to the interview.

Claire also interviewed a young student who lives in London. Her name is Lorraine Taylor. This is what Lorraine told Claire:

I'm from Trinidad and I've been living here for two years. I came to London to study Hospital Management. In some ways I like it very much. In other ways I don't. For example, I think it's a very interesting city. I'm never bored here. And I think parts of London are really very beautiful. I love the big parks and some of the buildings. But I can't stand the weather. It rains so much here. And it's so noisy, too. So much traffic. So many cars everywhere. Of course, we have traffic problems in Trinidad. But not like this!

At first I was very lonely here. I was always home-sick. I didn't have any friends. Now I have a few. Not many. But a few. Things are better now. But I don't think I want to stay here. After I finish my course I intend to go back to Trinidad. Perhaps I can get a job there in Hospital Management. I hope so!

4 Claire asked Lorraine a lot of questions. What do you think they were?

1 Where ________?
2 How long ________?
3 Why ________?
4 Do ________?
5 What don't you ________?
6 How did you feel when ________?
7 Did you have ________?
8 How many ________?
9 What do you intend ________ after ________?

1 Stop and look.

<table>
<tr><td colspan="2">How long have you been</td><td colspan="2">living in ________?
working in/for ________?</td></tr>
<tr><td>I've been</td><td colspan="3">living in ________ for ________ years/months.
working here since 1979.</td></tr>
<tr><td>She's been
He's</td><td colspan="2">living in London
working in that factory</td><td>for a long time now.
since 19 ________.</td></tr>
</table>

Write:

I *have* been ________ ing

He | *has* been ________ ing
She |

Say:

I'*ve* |
He'*s* | been ________ ing
She'*s* |

Remember! We use this form only when we are still working or living in the place!

2 Write about Gavin Cass.

1 Gavin ________ born in Inverness but he has ________ living in Killbrae for more ________ fifty years.
2 He ________ the village ________ very beautiful but he doesn't ________ the people are very friendly.
3 He doesn't really like them very ________.

These are the missing words. Where do they belong?
thinks, think, been, much, is, was, than

3 Write about Lorraine Taylor, too.

1 Lorraine __(1)__ from Trinidad. She __(2)__ born there.
2 She __(3)__ been __(4)__ in London __(5)__ two years.
3 There are things she __(6)__ about London and things she __(7)__ like.
4 For example, she __(8)__ the big parks but she can't __(9)__ the weather.
5 For a long time she didn't have very __(10)__ friends in London but she has a __(11)__ now.

These are the missing words. Where do they belong? Which word is used twice?
a) doesn't b) has c) many d) few e) likes f) for g) was h) living i) stand j) is

4 Finding out what other people think.

What do you think of ________? What's ________ like? What are ________ like?

Claire also interviewed a factory worker who lives in Stockport. His name is Ted. Look at his answers. What are Claire's questions?

CLAIRE: ________?
TED: For ten years now.
CLAIRE: ________?
TED: Oh, I don't think it's so bad. Not really.
CLAIRE: ________?
TED: The people? Oh, they're very friendly.
CLAIRE: ________?
TED: The weather? Terrible! It's even worse than it is in London!

Unit Six

E

1

2 3 4

1 Which advertisement goes with which picture?

a Charming cottage in the country. Good roof and outside walls but needs some decoration inside. Large, pleasant garden. A real bargain!

b Luxury flat on top floor of high building with fine view of sea. One bedroom. Basement garage. Close to station and motorway. One hour to London. All mod cons.

c Large family house in quiet suburb. Close to good shops and school. Kitchen, dining room and living room downstairs. Three bedrooms and bathroom upstairs. Gas central heating. Small garden and garage.

d Furnished room in small flat in centre of London. Share bathroom and kitchen with two music students. Low rent. Sorry no pets.

2 Speak and write.

Describe each of the four places in full sentences, like this (example for picture one): This is a luxury flat on the top floor of a . . . . It has . . .

3 What do you think?

These people are looking for somewhere to live. Which of the four places above do you think is best for them? Why?

Mr and Mrs Bailey both work, have three children and a dog. They have very little free time.

Bernard Wheaton, an artist who hates cities, has very little money but is good with his hands.

Dave Martin, a young photographer with a job in London. Earns very little.

Jennifer Walker, has a very good job in London, drives a fast sports car, single, travels a lot. Good salary. Rich father. Likes swimming and sunbathing.

THE VISITOR

EPISODE SIX

Tony Redford is a journalist. Yesterday a strange woman phoned him. She asked him to meet her in a pub called 'The Brunswick'.

The next evening Tony was in *The Brunswick*.
'Who can she be? Why is she interested in Shandor?' he thought. At exactly nine o'clock, a tall, thin woman with short dark hair walked in. She looked around the pub and then came over to Tony.
'Good evening. Are you Mr Redford?' she asked.
'Yes, that's right. Are you the woman who . . .?' She nodded.
'I hope you haven't been waiting long. Please . . . I have very little time. And I have very many questions to ask you.' She looked around the pub. It was very crowded. She and Tony sat down at a table in the corner, far away from the other people.

She began at once.
'In your article you mention Thomas Shandor and his company. But you say very little about exactly what his company makes. Is it perhaps some kind of electronic brain? A very small one? Better than any other electronic brain?' Tony stared at her in surprise.
'How did you know about that? It's one of the company's most important secrets!' The woman didn't answer for a moment.
'I've been studying the electronics industry of your country for a long time.' Again Tony noticed her careful, very correct English. It was almost perfect.
'Where do you come from?' he asked.
'I am a visitor to your country.'
'That isn't an answer to my question!'

Suddenly the woman turned and looked around the pub. For a moment she looked like a cat who senses danger. Then she looked back at him. She spoke in a low voice.
'Please, you must believe me. I am a friend. I want to help you. But I need your help, too. Where did you get your information about Shandor? You must tell me! Please!'
Tony thought for a moment and then told her about Presley, the engineer who worked in Shandor's factory in Southampton.
'But he didn't tell me very much. He died in an accident two days ago.'
'An accident? What kind of accident?' Tony told her about it.
They didn't notice the man who sat far away from them, on the other side of the pub, reading a newspaper. He was very tall and he wore strange, round glasses. He listened to Tony and the tall young woman and could understand every word they said. And his eyes were more than eyes. He could see through the newspaper. He sat there, and listened and watched.

Questions.

1 What is strange about the woman?
2 What is strange about the tall man?
3 Which one of them do you think works for Shandor?

Unit Seven

A

Good evening. This is Claire Walton again with *The News in Focus*. Our two stories again come from the headlines in today's papers.

MAN GETS MEMORY BACK AFTER TEN YEARS
BETTER WEATHER ON THE WAY AT LAST

One Saturday morning David Young went out to buy his wife a birthday present. He promised to come back in a few hours. But he didn't. In fact, Mrs Young has been waiting for him and that birthday present ever since.

But late last night the telephone rang in Mrs Young's home in South London. For the first time in ten years she heard her husband's voice again. Where has Mr Young been all this time? What happened to him that day ten years ago? And where was he last night when he phoned his wife? You'll get the answers to these questions later in the programme.

1

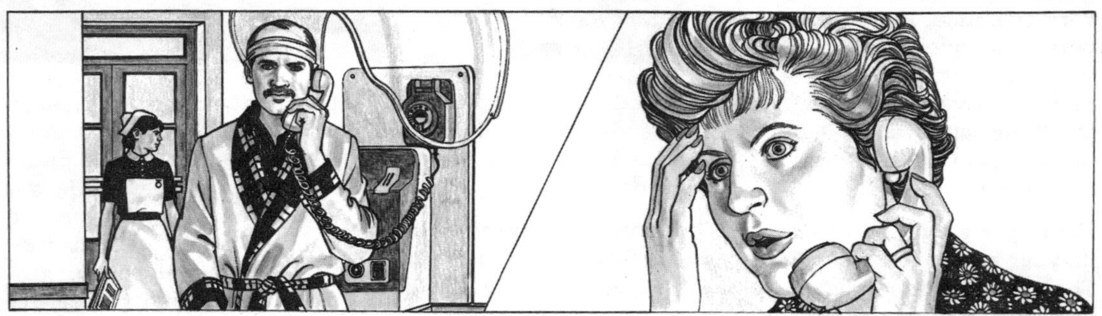

2

Our other story this evening is the weather. For the last five days it has been below zero in most parts of the country. Cold, frost and heavy snow have caused terrible problems everywhere. Everyone is asking the same question – 'When will it end?'

Well, the weatherman predicts it won't last much longer. Better weather is on the way. The temperature will rise above zero tomorrow. And we'll see the sun again for a few hours. There'll be more about this, too, in our special weather report at the end of the programme.

B

Look at the two headlines and answer these questions:

a What do you think happened to the man ten years ago?
b What is the weather like *now*?

Answer.

Picture one

1 Why did Mr Young go out?
2 What didn't he do?
3 How many years has Mrs Young been waiting for him?
4 What happened last night?
5 What questions do you think Mrs Young asked him?
6 What will happen later in the programme?

Picture two

1 What has the weather been like?
2 What exactly is the question everyone is asking?
3 What does the weatherman predict?
4 What will the weather be like tomorrow?

1 Stop and look.

1 It has been cold **for** five days.

MONDAY TUESDAY WEDNESDAY THURSDAY FRIDAY

It has been cold **since** last Monday.

Use *for* when you are talking about a length of time. (————) *Five days, ten years, three hours* are all lengths of time.
Use *since* when you point back to the point in time (←———) when something began.

2 Use *since* or *for*.

1 It is eleven o'clock. The man has been waiting for the bus ________ 10.30.
2 In other words, he has been there ________ half an hour.
3 The woman has been waiting ________ only ten minutes.
4 In other words, she has been waiting ________ 10.50.
5 The man has been waiting ________ a longer time than the woman.

3 Read and answer.

When *will* the cold weather stop? It *won't* go on much longer.

Will and *won't* (the short form for *will not*) are another way of talking about the future. We use *will* a lot when we make predictions about the future. The weatherman makes predictions about the weather.
For example, what do you think are the missing words here?

1 Do you think it ________ rain tomorrow?
2 Well, the weatherman says it ________ rain, so we can go on a picnic if you want to.
3 Tomorrow ________ be a fine day. It ________ be very warm.
4 There ________ be a little rain but it probably ________ fall here in the south.
5 In other words, it ________ fall only in the north and east.
6 The west ________ have a good day without rain, too.

Unit Seven

C

1 This is part of a newspaper article about Mr Young.

Mrs Young didn't know that her husband wanted to buy a present for her. He said he wanted to go for a walk. But he took a train into the centre of London instead. Then he went to Oxford Street. He says he wanted to buy the present at one of the big stores there. But when he was in Oxford Street, a bus knocked him down. And this had a very strange result. When he woke up in hospital he couldn't remember anything, not even his name. He didn't have any identification on him so nobody knew who he was.

Ten years went by. In those ten years Mr Young started a new life. He took a new name and found a new job. He also met another woman, Nancy Lewis. He promised to marry Miss Lewis. He was on his way to church to marry her last week when he had another accident. This time he ran into a lorry in his car. He hit his head in the accident and woke up in hospital again. Suddenly he could remember everything again. He remembered his old name, his address and, most important of all, the fact that he was already married. He phoned his wife from hospital, and tried to explain everything. He also phoned Miss Lewis. Both women refuse to believe his story. They both think he is lying.

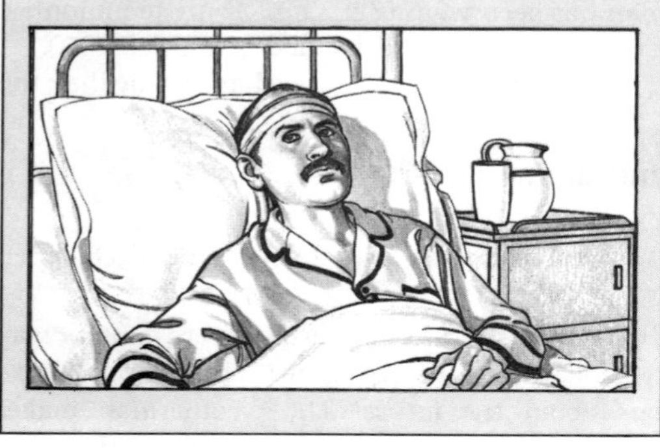

2 Answer these questions.

1 What did Mr Young tell his wife?
2 What did he really do?
3 Why?
4 Explain what happened to him then.
5 What about the next ten years?
6 Why didn't he marry Miss Lewis?
7 What did he do in hospital?
8 What do the two women think?
9 What do you think?

3 This is part of the conversation between Mr Young and Miss Lewis. What are the missing words?

NANCY: You can't marry me? What do you ___(1)___

MR YOUNG: I can't because I'm ___(2)___ already.

NANCY: What? Why didn't you ___(3)___ me that before?

MR YOUNG: Because I forgot.

NANCY: You forgot? Is this a joke? Because it isn't funny! How can you ___(4)___ something like that?

MR YOUNG: Let me ___(5)___. ___(6)___ me a chance.

NANCY: All right. Explain it. I'm waiting.

MR YOUNG: Well, you see, ten years ___(7)___ I ___(8)___ an accident. A bus ___(9)___ me down and when I ___(10)___ up in hospital, I couldn't ___(11)___ anything, not even my name.

NANCY: I don't ___(12)___ a word you're saying. Why are you ___(13)___ these terrible lies?

MR YOUNG: No, no. I'm not ___(14)___. It's the ___(15)___!

Here are the missing words. Where do they belong?

a) tell b) explain c) believe d) mean
e) ago f) telling g) had h) forget
i) woke j) truth k) married l) Give
m) remember n) lying o) ran

4 Listen to the full conversation on tape.

1 Mr Young promised to come home at six. What did he say?

a I must come home at six.
b I'll come home at six.
c I should come home at six.
d I come home at six.

2 Look at the three pictures. In each one someone is making a promise. What do you think they are promising to do (or not to do)?

Here are the three promises. But who is saying them? In which picture?

a Thanks a lot. I'll pay you back tomorrow.
b I'm sorry I hit him, sir. I won't do it again.
c I'll always love you! I'll never leave you!

3 Find the conversation.

This is what Mr Young said to Mrs Young one Saturday morning ten years ago. This is her part of the conversation. Find his part of the conversation.

1 Where are you going, David?
2 Oh? Why?
3 When will you be back?
4 Well, don't be late. Remember that we're having lunch at one o'clock.
5 Oh, by the way, I need some tea from the supermarket. Could you get some for me?
6 Bye! Have a nice walk.

a In a few hours.
b Yes, I'll get some on my way back from the park.
c To the park.
d Bye!
e Because I'd like to take a walk and get some fresh air.
f I won't forget. Don't worry.

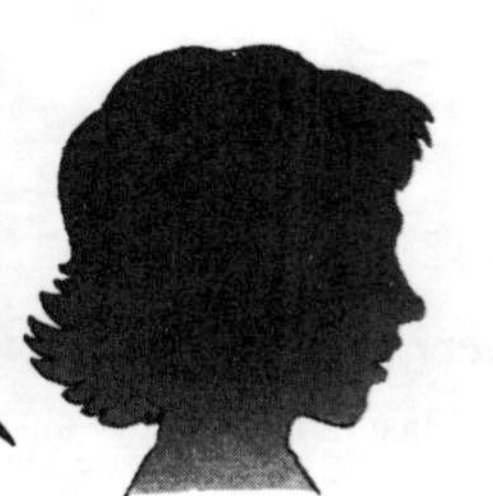

4 Listen to the conversation on tape.

Unit Seven

E

1 The weather report.

And now for that special weather report we promised you. First, let's look at the weather in the last 24 hours. The coldest part of the country has been the north of Scotland. The temperature there was 4 degrees below zero at midnight last night. This morning it was bright and sunny there and still very cold. In the east of Scotland there was heavy snow again but it was a bit warmer, with the temperature about 2 degrees below freezing. Here in England the maximum temperature was 1 degree above zero in London. The minimum was 1 degree below in Manchester. It has been a cloudy day in most parts, with a cold wind. But it hasn't rained, except in the west. There was very heavy rain there this morning. But this has stopped now.

Well, what about the outlook for the next 24 hours? In most parts of England the temperature will be 2 or 3 degrees above zero, at least during the day. But at night it will fall below zero again, so there will still be some ice on the roads. Most of Scotland will have a very cold, dry day, with temperatures just below zero. In the east, in the area around Aberdeen, it will be warmer, but it will probably snow there. This snow could be very heavy in places. It's also going to be a windy day in most parts of the country, particularly on the eastern and north-eastern coasts of both Scotland and England.

Well, that's the outlook. And that's all from me, too, until tomorrow.

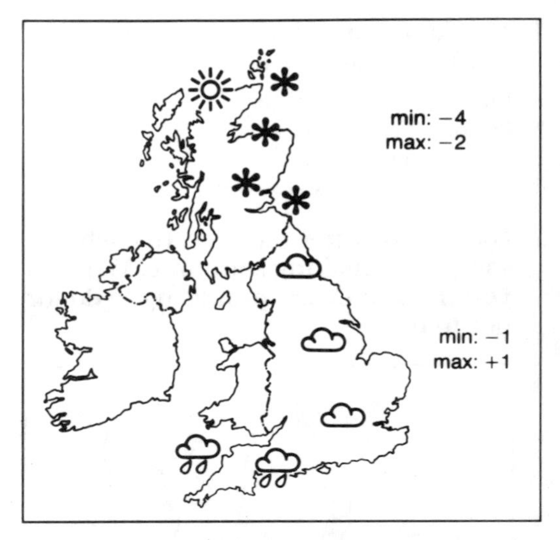

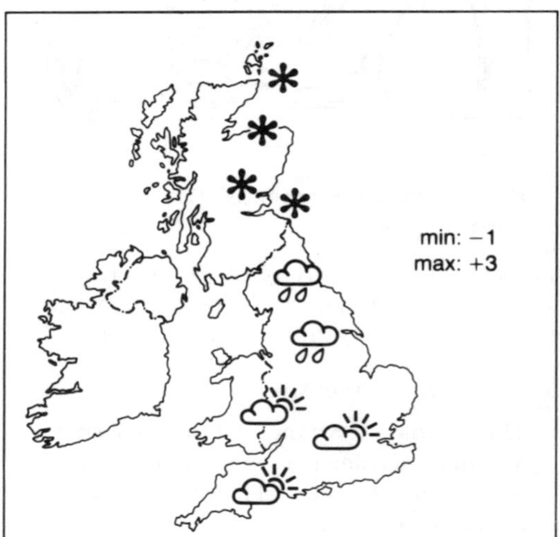

2 Answer.

1 Where has it been:
  a coldest?
  b warmest?
  c cloudy?
  d sunny?

2 Has it rained anywhere today?

3 What about the weather?

Describe the weather in the last 24 hours where you are.

4 Ask and answer questions about the weather in:

a the east of Scotland.
b the rest of Scotland.
c the north of England.
d the west of England.

e.g. Will it ________ in ________? Yes, it will. / No, it won't.

5 Now predict the weather in the next 24 hours where you are:

I think it'll probably ________.

THE VISITOR

EPISODE SEVEN

Tony Redford, a journalist, is talking to a woman in a pub. They don't know that a tall man with round glasses is listening to them.

They left the pub and began to walk towards Tony's flat.
'I don't even know your name,' Tony said. She suddenly turned and looked behind her.
'You can call me Tan-Lin,' she answered.
'What kind of name is that? And what nationality are you?' he asked. But she didn't answer. She looked behind her again and then began to walk faster. They came to a busy street.
'We can cross at the traffic lights,' Tony said.
'No, let's walk along this street a little,' she said. He followed her. Halfway along the street, where there were no traffic lights, she stopped. Then she began to cross the road.
'Don't do that. It's dangerous!' he shouted. But he ran after her. A car almost hit them. She jumped aside, like a cat, and pulled him with her. When they were on the other side, she looked back at the traffic lights again.
'You shouldn't cross a busy road like this in the middle! Why did you do it?' Tony asked. He looked back at the lights, too, and saw a tall man with round glasses. The man stood there, looking up and down.
'Do you know that man?' she asked Tony.
'No, I don't think so. Why?'
She didn't answer for a moment.
'There's something about him I don't like,' she finally said.

She walked so fast it was difficult to keep up with her. She turned into a narrow side street and then walked into an alley that led to another street.
'You know these streets better than I do,' Tony said.
'But you live around here, don't you?' she asked. Tony looked at her.
'How do you know so much about me? And why do you want to know so much about people like Shandor?' he asked. She turned down another narrow street and looked behind. The tall man with round glasses was no longer behind them.
'I can't answer your questions now. But I will later. I promise. And you must promise me something,' she said.
'What?'
'Be careful, Mr Redford. You should be *very* careful. Shandor is more dangerous than you think. And he is planning to build something far more important than an electronic brain. Perhaps he has built it already.'
'What do you mean?' he asked.
'I mean that Shandor can probably build robots that look and act like human beings. Perhaps he can even build exact copies of people. Exact copies of you and me!'
He wanted to ask her more but she left him with the words: 'Remember. Be careful. Very careful. You'll hear from me in a few days!'

Questions.

1. Why do you think Tan-Lin walked so fast?
2. Have you any ideas about who she is and what she wants to do?
3. Why do you think Tony should be careful?

Unit Eight

A

Hello again. Our theme this week is *travel*. Do you travel a lot? And do you enjoy it? Here is what four people said.

I travel all over the world. I get pretty tired of it sometimes. I fly everywhere. Sometimes I don't even know which country I'm in. I wake up in a hotel and wonder where I am. One hotel is just like another. It doesn't matter where you are. *Eric Cook*

I wouldn't say I travel a lot. I go to Paris on business sometimes and my husband and I usually go away on holiday every year. Last year we went to Hong Kong. I think it's good to travel and see other places. But I don't like package tours. And I think it's better to speak the language. That always helps. *Eileen Chase*

I don't travel very much but I'd like to. I've only been to France and Spain. I really enjoyed it. My boyfriend and I went on our bikes. And sometimes we used public transport – trains and buses. I think that's the best way to travel. By public transport or bike. You see more and you don't get into traffic jams. *Jill Reed*

Travel? I hate it! I've only been abroad once. We went to Italy. It was the wife's idea, not mine. I couldn't find a good cup of tea anywhere. And no fish and chips, either! All those foreigners! I couldn't understand a word they said. I'll never do it again. I'd prefer to stay at home and watch the telly. *Arnold Blunt*

Answer.

1 Talk about some of the places you'd like to travel to.
2 Why would you like to go there? What would you like to see and do there?

Picture one

1 Do you think Eric Cook enjoys travelling? Why? (or why not?)

Picture two

1 Where has Jill been?
2 How did she go there?
3 What about you? Where have you been?
4 How did you go there?

Picture three

1 Where does Eileen Chase go sometimes?
2 Why?
3 What does she say about travel? What do you think?

Picture four

1 Why do you think Arnold Blunt doesn't enjoy travelling?

1 Stop and look.

Talking about how you get to work or to school:

I usually go *by*	bus. car. train.
Sometimes I go	*on* foot. *on* my bike. *in* my car.

2 How do you travel?

Most of us travel in more than one way. By car, on foot, etc. What about you? Describe two or three of the ways you travel to work, school and other places.

3 Stop and look.

Talking about how long it takes:

It usually *takes me*	10 minutes an hour a few minutes	to get to	work. school. the office.

4 Ask and answer.

How long does it usually take you

to	go to school? get to work? have breakfast in the morning? etc.

5 Finish these sentences about Jill Reed.

1 Jill was late ________ work yesterday.
2 She usually goes to work ________ her bike.
3 But yesterday she ________ the bus.
4 It usually ________ her about 20 minutes to ________ to work.
5 But yesterday it ________ her 40 minutes.
6 The bus got ________ a traffic jam.
7 She sat in the bus for ten minutes and then got ________.
8 She went the rest of the way ________ foot.
9 That was why she was ________ for work.
10 Sometimes she goes to work ________ train, too.
11 She prefers to ________ by train because it is always faster.

Unit Eight

C

1 Listen and answer.

Here are three different conversations. Two of them are in a travel agency. One of them is at the British Rail travel office at Victoria (a big London station).

Conversation 1.

WOMAN: What exactly does the price include?
CLERK: Return air fare to Los Angeles, accommodation, and a guided tour of Disneyland.
WOMAN: What kind of accommodation?
CLERK: Room with bath in a second class hotel.
WOMAN: What about meals?
CLERK: Only breakfast is included in the price.
WOMAN: Hmm . . . I'd like to think about it.
CLERK: Certainly. Would you like a brochure?
WOMAN: Yes, please.

Conversation 2.

MAN: I'd like some information about the trains to Hove, please. It's a town near Brighton and . . .
CLERK: Yes, sir. I know where it is. When did you want to go?
MAN: Tomorrow. I have to be there before 11.30. You see, I . . .
CLERK: There's a fast train at 10.08. It'll get you there at 11.20. But you have to change at Brighton.
MAN: Change at Brighton? Isn't there a through train?
CLERK: Yes, there's one at 10.27. But that doesn't get in until 11.39.
MAN: Oh, that's too late. Could you repeat that information about the first train, please? When does it leave?

Conversation 3.

WOMAN: How do we get from the airport to the town centre?
CLERK: It's probably best to take a taxi.
MAN: Isn't there a bus?
CLERK: Yes, but the plane won't arrive until after midnight. The bus probably stops running before that.
WOMAN: How much do you think the taxi will cost?
CLERK: I'm afraid I don't know. But it won't be too much. Taxis are very cheap in Portugal. And it isn't far from the airport to the town centre.

1 What are they talking about?
2 What will the woman get for the price?
3 What won't she get?
4 Is she definitely going?

5 Where does the man want to go?
6 When?
7 What's wrong with the first train?
8 What's wrong with the second one?
9 Which one do you think the man will take?
10 Why?

11 Where do you think the man and woman are going?
12 What's the problem?
13 What doesn't the clerk know?
14 What does he think they should do?
15 Why?

Unit Eight

D

1 This timetable shows some of the trains between Hove (a place very near Brighton) and London. Study the timetable and the notes, then answer the questions.

		(sx)						(so)
Hove	dep.	6.20	6.40	7.26	7.40	8.26	8.40	9.10
Brighton	arr.	6.25	....	7.31	....	8.31	....	....
	dep.	6.30	....	7.36	....	8.36	....	....
London	arr.	7.28	7.42	8.34	8.42	9.34	9.44	10.14

Notes so: Saturdays only
sx: This train does not run on Saturdays

1 You want a through train to London from Hove. Which trains can you catch?
2 What do you have to do if you catch the other trains?
3 What does the timetable tell you about Saturdays?
4 What exactly do *dep.* and *arr.* mean?

2 Stop and look.

> If I *take* the 7.26, when *will* I arrive in London?

Ask the same question about the: 7.40, 8.26, 8.40.

> If you *take* the 6.20, you'*ll* arrive in London at 7.28.

Make at least four more sentences like this about the other trains on the timetable.

3 Make more sentences like these, with different words.

Example: (*arrive, take*) When you ________ in Los Angeles, a bus ________ you to the hotel.
= When you arrive in Los Angeles, a bus will take you to the hotel.

1 (*leave, catch*) If you ________ now, you ________ your train.
2 (*phone, get*) My friend ________ you when he ________ to London.
3 (*do, understand*) If you ________ this exercise, you ________ the difference between *when* and *if*.
4 (*ask, have*) I ________ the teacher if I ________ trouble.

Unit Eight

E

1 Eileen Chase tells a story about modern travel. Has anything like this ever happened to you?

Last winter I went to New York on business. My husband came with me. On the fifth and last day we packed our bags and checked out of the hotel in the morning. My husband decided to do some more sightseeing while I was at another business meeting. We agreed to meet at the airport that evening. We had to be there by eight o'clock at the latest. Our plane was due to leave at a quarter past nine.

The meeting went on and on! I stayed until about a quarter past six. Then I had to apologise and leave. When I got down to the street below, there was heavy snow everywhere. I caught a taxi but it was just before Christmas and there was a terrible traffic jam. We crawled along. I looked at my watch again and again. I was very worried. I didn't want to miss my plane! Then the taxi broke down. Suddenly I remembered something. There's a subway service – that's what the Americans call their underground trains – to the airport. I ran to the nearest station. It was almost seven when I got there. I had to go to another station and change trains once. That took more than a quarter of an hour. Then I had to wait another ten minutes before the right train came. It took another hour to get to a station near the airport, where we had to change again. But this time we took a bus the rest of the way. It was almost eight-thirty.

It wasn't far to the airport but the snow was heavier and so was the traffic. Much heavier! When I finally got to the airport, it was almost nine. I hurried off the bus with all my baggage and ran towards the check-in desk. Then I fell and almost broke my ankle. There was a big crowd of people around the check-in desk. One of them was my husband. He helped me to get up.

'There was no need to hurry,' he said. 'This snow has delayed everything. The plane's late, too.'

2 Ask and answer.

Finish the questions:

1 How long did they stay in ________?
2 What did she do on the last ________?
3 Did he go to a business ________, too?
4 Where did they arrange to ________?
5 When did she finally leave the ________?

Now ask some more questions with words like:
Did ________? Why ________? Was ________?
How long did it take to ________? etc.

WHAT PEOPLE SAY

Now turn to page 104 and listen to the tape to find out what people say about their holidays.

THE VISITOR

EPISODE EIGHT

Yesterday evening Tony Redford met a strange woman in a pub. They talked about Shandor. Later, a man with round glasses followed them.

The next morning Tony left his flat, as usual, at eight o'clock. He always travelled to work on the Underground. As he walked to the station, he thought about his meeting with the strange woman.
'Why didn't she answer me when I asked her about her nationality? Is her name really Tan-Lin? And is it possible that Shandor can make robots that act and talk like human beings?' These were some of the questions in his mind. He thought about them as he stood on the crowded platform.
'The service isn't very good this morning,' someone next to him said.
'No, it's getting worse and worse. I've been waiting for a train for ten minutes now!' someone else answered. But Tony didn't listen to the conversations around him. And he didn't notice the tall man with round glasses just behind him in the crowd.

Tony was on the edge of the platform. He could hear the sound of a train approaching in the tunnel.
'Thank God, one's coming now! At last!' someone said. Tony stepped closer to the edge and looked down the tunnel. As the train came nearer, he stepped back a little. But it was difficult to stand away from the edge because there were so many people behind him. Suddenly he felt something in his back. He thought it was a hand but he couldn't be sure. Whatever it was, it pushed him back towards the edge. Then, with the train approaching very fast, it pushed again, very hard.

Tony fell in front of the train. But somehow, as he did so, he grabbed the edge of the platform. And as he fell, he pulled his body inwards, away from the electric rail and towards the base of the platform below. At this moment, he looked up and saw the big steel wheels of the train. They came closer and closer. There was a squealing of brakes as the driver tried to stop the train. Someone screamed.

'What's happened?' someone else shouted.
'A man is down there!' another voice said.
'He jumped in front of the train!' In the shouting and screaming, nobody noticed the tall man with round glasses. He walked away and up the steps. His job was done. He didn't wait to see the body of the young journalist.

It took the firemen and the police half an hour to free Tony. The man with round glasses didn't know that in many Underground stations in London, there is a gap between the rail and the base of the platform. The gap is just big enough for a thin man or woman. As he lay there, in that gap, Tony thought again and again of Tan-Lin's warning. 'Be careful. Be very careful!'

Questions.

1 Why did Tony fall?
2 What happened after he fell?
3 What does the tall man with round glasses think?

Unit Nine

A

Hello. This is Claire Walton with another *The News in Focus*. Here are the headlines for this evening's stories.

LIGHTNING STRIKES AIRLINER THREE TIMES
THRILLING FINISH IN BIG RACE
POP STAR TO BEGIN NEW CAREER IN FILMS

1

Early this morning an airliner with 300 passengers left London for Australia. But only ten minutes after take-off, it had to turn back. In a terrifying storm, lightning struck the airliner at least three times. One of the petrol tanks caught fire. But somehow the pilot landed the plane safely. Later in the programme we talk to him and to two of the passengers.

This afternoon two of the fastest and most famous runners in the world met in the 3,000 metres race here in London. A crowd of more than 90,000 watched Sebastiano Ovetti and Steve Coles in the thrilling contest. At least 2,000 more people were very disappointed because they couldn't get into the stadium. Ovetti was in the lead until the last 200 metres. Then Coles came up from behind. What happened then? Find out later in the programme.

2

Do you remember this face? Judy Garrett used to be one of Europe's most popular singers. But Judy hasn't been very happy lately. Her last few records haven't been very successful. And now Judy plans to start a new career. She is going to begin a film in Hollywood in the next few days. This isn't her first part in films. She has sung and danced in them before. But this time Judy is going to have a very serious part. We interview her later in the programme. She tells us all about her new film.

3

Answer.

One of the three headlines is about something that is going to happen. Which one?

Picture one

1 Why did the airliner turn back?
2 What do you think the pilot is going to talk about?
3 How do you think he feels now? Why?

Picture two

1 What can you find out later in the programme?
2 Why do you think some people were disappointed?
3 Who exactly are Coles and Ovetti?

Picture three

1 Why hasn't Judy been very happy lately?
2 What kind of roles has she had in films before?
3 What is different about this film?

1 Stop and look.

Look at these two headlines. One is past. One is future. Which?

PLANE TURNS BACK IN TERRIBLE STORM
JUDY GARRETT TO STAR IN NEW FILM

The second headline means:
Judy Garrett will star in a new film *or* Judy Garrett is going to star in a new film. (Both future forms are possible here.)

What do these headlines mean?

1 WORLD LEADERS TO MEET NEXT MONTH IN PARIS
2 FAMOUS ATHLETE TO HAVE BABY
3 QUEEN TO VISIT AUSTRALIA
4 GAS PRICES TO GO UP 10%
5 FILM STAR TO MARRY AGAIN

2 Read and answer.

The plane *had to* turn back.

A lot of people *couldn't* get into the stadium.

These are the past forms of *have to* and *can*. This is what a radio reporter said at the stadium. Rewrite the report in the past.

Example: It is a warm afternoon in London.
= It was a warm afternoon in London.

1 More than 90,000 people are in the stadium.
2 Many of them can't find seats.
3 Thousands have to stand.
4 Some can't really see the race.
5 And the stadium is so big that a lot of people have to use binoculars.
6 But even they can't see very much.
7 Some people have to pay very high prices for a ticket.
8 You can't get a ticket for under £40.
9 Thousands more have to wait outside the stadium.
10 I just can't believe there are so many people here!
11 I have to stop! I have to get some fresh air!

Unit Nine

C

1 Listen to the interview.

Claire Walton interviews the pilot of the airliner and two passengers. One of them is Mrs Nora Williams. The other is her son, Billy.

CLAIRE: Captain Miles, could you tell us exactly what happened?

CAPTAIN MILES: Well, it was a very unusual storm. Of course it isn't unusual for lightning to strike a plane. But it is unusual when it strikes it three times.

CLAIRE: Is that why the petrol tank caught fire?

CAPTAIN MILES: Probably. We can't be sure yet. Perhaps there was another cause.

CLAIRE: How did you feel when all this happened?

CAPTAIN MILES: Well, I've been flying for more than twenty years. I've been in a lot of storms, but never one as bad as that . . . and . . . I was . . . worried. Very worried indeed.

CLAIRE: How did you feel, Mrs Williams? Were you afraid?

MRS WILLIAMS: Afraid? I was terrified! I've never been so terrified in my life! I can't tell you how glad I was when we landed safely. And I really want to compliment the pilot and the crew. They were wonderful! Really marvellous! They were so calm!

CLAIRE: How did you feel, Billy?

BILLY: Oh, I was excited. I've never seen a storm like that before. It was really great! And I was disappointed when we had to turn back.

CLAIRE: Disappointed? Why?

BILLY: I wanted to see more of the storm! I can't wait until tomorrow!

CLAIRE: Why? What's going to happen tomorrow?

BILLY: We're going to get on another plane. To Australia. And perhaps we'll see another storm again! I'm really looking forward to it!

2 Answer.

1 Was this the worst storm the captain has ever seen?
2 What does Mrs Williams say about it?
3 How did Billy feel?
4 Why?

3 Ask and answer.

Finish the questions. What are the answers?

1 How long ________ Captain Miles ________ flying?
2 Has he ________ in a lot of storms?
3 ________ he ever been in a storm like that before?
4 ________ Mrs Williams very afraid?
5 How ________ she feel when the plane landed?
6 ________ Billy terrified during the storm?

1 ***How do they feel?* Look at the situations.**

In which do you think someone is:

a disappointed?
b very surprised or astonished?
c terrified?

2 This is part of a newspaper article about the race.

Ovetti went into the lead very early in the race and stayed there until the last 200 metres. Then Coles made his move. The Englishman moved up just behind the Italian and then tried to pass him. But the Italian began to run faster. So did Coles. The crowd began to cheer wildly as the two came around the final bend, with Ovetti still in the lead. Then the Italian made a mistake which cost him the race. He looked round for a second to see where Coles was. Then he suddenly stumbled and fell. Coles went on to win the race in a new record time of 7:30.2.

After the race, Coles said,
'I just couldn't believe my eyes when Seb suddenly fell like that. I never expected to see that happen and I never wanted to win this way!'

Ovetti later told our reporter,
'I just don't know what happened. I was sure I could win. But the next thing I knew, there I was on the ground. I really feel terrible about it.'

3 Answer.

1 Who was in the lead most of the time?
2 Why did Ovetti lose the race?
3 How do you think Coles felt when Ovetti stumbled and fell?
4 How does Ovetti feel now? Why?

4 Ask and answer.

Use *surprised*, *excited* or *disappointed* in your questions:

1 Was the crowd very ________ when Coles and Ovetti came round the final bend?
2 Was Coles very ________ when Ovetti fell?
3 Is Ovetti very ________ because he lost the race?

Unit Nine

E

1 Find the dialogue.

On the left are the interviewer's questions. Find Judy's answer to each question (on the right).

1 Tell us about this new film which you're going to make. Is it a musical, Judy?
2 Oh? What kind of film is it, then?
3 What's it about?
4 And what's it called?
5 Why is it called that?
6 And when can I do that? I mean, when can we all see it?
7 Well, Judy, good luck! And I hope your new film will be very successful.

a 'The Bridge.'
b Thank you. I hope so too.
c It's due to come out early next year.
d A man and a woman who fall in love. They both have problems.
e It's a love story, really.
f Because they always meet on the same bridge in Paris. But if you want to find out more, go and see the film when it comes out.
g No, it isn't.

2 You can listen to the complete dialogue on tape.

3 *Who* or *Which?* That is the question!

Tell us about the new film *which* you're going to make. It's about a man and a woman *who* fall in love.

1 Which word (*who* or *which*) do you use for *people?*
2 Which word do you use for *things?*

4 Now use *who* or *which* in these sentences.

1 The first news story was about a plane ________ had to turn back in a terrible storm.
2 They talked to the pilot ________ landed the plane safely.
3 They also talked to a boy ________ enjoyed the storm.
4 A few years ago Judy made a musical ________ was a big success.
5 *The Bridge* is the first film in ________ she doesn't sing or dance.
6 She isn't the first pop star ________ has wanted to act in serious films.

THE VISITOR

EPISODE NINE

The story so far:
Tony Redford is a young journalist. He is trying to find out more about a strange engineer and owner of a factory. This man's name is Thomas Shandor. Nobody knows very much about him.
Yesterday, someone tried to kill Tony Redford as he waited for an Underground train. But Tony did not die. Harlan works for Shandor. He often goes to see Shandor on his yacht.

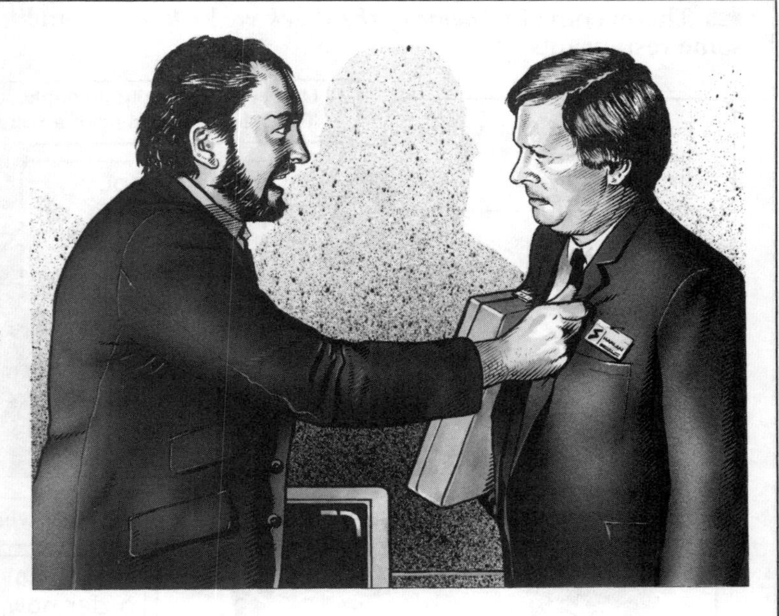

Harlan was a worried man that morning. As soon as the helicopter landed, he hurried to Shandor's cabin.
'I'm very disappointed, Harlan!' Shandor said. Harlan saw more than disappointment in those cold blue eyes. There was anger there. In fact, Shandor was furious.
'I'm sorry, Mr Shandor. Let me explain,' Harlan began. But Shandor stopped him.
'I'm not interested in your explanations. I want to know only one thing. Why isn't Redford dead? Didn't you follow my orders?' Shandor controlled the fury in his voice. But the look in his eye became colder.

'Yes, of course I did, Mr Shandor. The operator had to choose a good place to kill Redford. And he did. We instructed him to leave the place as soon as possible. He did this, too. He followed all our instructions.'
'Then why didn't he kill Redford?' Shandor asked coldly.
'Because the operator had no imagination.'
'No imagination? What do you mean?' For the first time, Shandor shouted at Harlan.
'Because the operator's computer calculated that Redford must be dead. And the operator couldn't imagine that something could be wrong with the calculations. That's what happens when these things have computers instead of real brains!'
Harlan stopped. He was frightened. Harlan didn't usually speak to Shandor like this.

Shandor thought for a moment. He was still very angry but not as angry as before.
'I'm still not satisfied with your explanation. But I will think about it. We must find another time and place to kill Redford.'
'And what about the woman, Mr Shandor? We still don't know who she is.' Shandor suddenly looked very worried.
'I will think about that, too,' he said. Harlan waited for a moment. Then he took some documents from his grey briefcase.
'I also have the new plans, Mr Shandor.' Shandor stopped thinking about the woman. He smiled.
'Ah, yes. The new plans. This time there must be no mistakes. Let me see them.'
'No, there won't be any mistakes tomorrow, Mr Shandor,' Harlan said. He tried to smile, too.

Unit Ten

A

This evening in *Theme of the Week* we look at the quality of food and service we get in some restaurants.

Unit Ten

Answer.

Pictures one – three

1 Why did they stop?
2 Why did they decide to go in?
3 What was it like inside?
4 So what exactly did Tony say to two people at that table for four?

Pictures four – six

1 What was the service like?
2 What did Helen want?
3 Why didn't she get it?
4 So what did she do?
5 What about Tony?

Pictures seven – nine

1 What did they have to do after they ordered?
2 What was the food like?
3 And what about the bill?

What do you think they should do now?
What do you think they are going to say?

Unit Ten

B

1 In which of these pictures do you think the woman is saying these things?

a The food smells good.
b It looks good.
c It tastes good.

2 Stop and look.

The food It	smells looks tastes	good. bad. strange. terrible. wonderful. delicious.
The vegetables They	smell look taste	

3 Use *It smells/looks/tastes* in these situations.

1 You are in the kitchen. You can see the food. 'Wonderful,' you think.
2 The food is in your mouth and it is terrible.
3 You aren't eating and you can't see the food but there is a good smell in the air. It is the food.

4 Read and answer.

Tony asks Helen:

> I wonder where the waiter is?

Of course, she doesn't know. Later, Tony says to Helen:

> I wonder where our steaks are?

Again it is difficult for her to answer.

We often ask questions with 'I wonder . . .?' when the person we are asking perhaps doesn't know the answer either.

Begin these questions with 'I wonder . . .?' What happens to them?

1 Is that table free?
2 Where are our steaks?
3 Where is the menu?
4 Has the waiter seen us?
5 Where's the food?
6 Will it come soon?
7 How much will the bill be?

5 Asking permission.

> May we sit here?
> May I have your order?

This is one way you can ask *permission* to do something. For example:

1 You are in a train. It is very hot. You want to open the window. What do you say to the person next to you?
2 You are at a friend's house and you want to use the phone. What do you say to your friend?
3 The door to your boss's office is open. You want to come in. What do you say when you knock?
4 You want to leave before the lesson ends. How do you ask the teacher for *permission* to do this?

Unit Ten

C

1 What's wrong with it?

This is the bill that Tony and Helen got. What do you think is wrong with it? Check it. Add the figures!

Harper's

76 Hawthorn Street, Hoddesdon, Herts. Tel: 23781

2 steaks	10·50
vegetables (2)	2·00
1 cheesecake	1·10
1 ice cream	·90
2 red wines	1·20
2 coffees	1·00
	18·90
10% service charge	3·00
	24·80

2 What is missing from this dialogue?

Helen is talking to the waiter about the bill. What are the missing words?

HELEN: Excuse me but I think you've ___(1)___ a mistake in the bill.
WAITER: What ___(2)___ of mistake?
HELEN: You've ___(3)___ us. Look, these figures are ___(4)___. They ___(5)___ add up.
WAITER: Where? I can't ___(6)___ any mistake.
HELEN: ___(7)___ you? Well, for example, this ___(8)___ here isn't right. You've ___(9)___ £18.90, but it ___(10)___ be £16.70!
WAITER: Oh . . . uh, yes, I see. ___(11)___ right.
HELEN: And ___(12)___ also ___(13)___ another mistake with the service charge. In fact, the whole ___(14)___ is wrong.
WAITER: Oh, I'm very ___(15)___.

These are the missing words. One of them is used more than once, which one?
a) don't b) you've c) you're d) made e) kind f) thing g) sorry h) overcharged i) find j) figure k) wrong l) put m) Can't n) must

3 You can listen to the dialogue, too.

D

1 Find the text!

This is part of an article about a restaurant in London. The sentences on the left are in order. Finish them with a sentence on the right.

1 *Annie's Bistro* is a small, friendly place. The food is very simple but very
2 To start with I had a salad of raw vegetables with a dressing of
3 My companion ordered a clear vegetable soup. She found it
4 To follow we both tried American pot roast. This is a beef dish, cooked
5 If you are interested in good value for money rather than fancy labels, try

a rather salty but at least it was home-made and not from a tin or a packet.
b the house red wine, which is good, honest and not too expensive.
c olive oil and lemon juice, with a little garlic and some herbs.
d good. It is owned and run by Annie Hill, an American from Boston, Massachusetts.
e in the oven with onions and carrots, in its own juice. It was delicious and tender!

Unit Ten

E

1 An old Dorset recipe.

Restaurants like *Annie's Bistro* specialise in simple but good dishes from England, America and France. One of the things you can get there is Dorset Beef in Cider. This is the recipe:

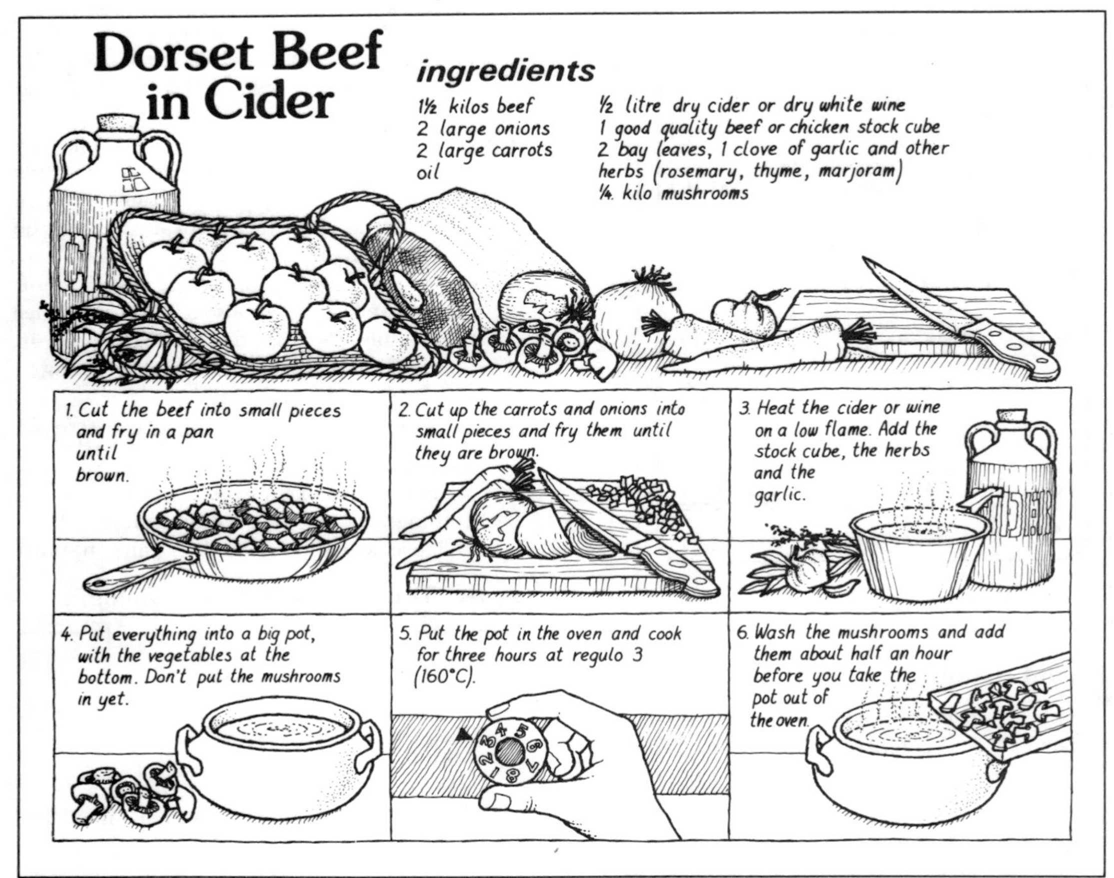

2 This is Annie Hill. She cooked this dish for some of her friends at home yesterday. Describe what she did.

1 First she ________ the beef into small ________.
2 Then she fried ________ in a ________ for a ________ minutes.
3 After that she ________ and fried them, too.
4 Then she ________ $\frac{1}{2}$ litre of cider on a ________ flame and ________ the stock cube, ________.
5 Next she ________ into a big ________ with the ________ at the ________.

Now go on. Finish the description of what she did.

THE VISITOR

EPISODE TEN

Carl Eastwood was a happy, friendly man. He had a good job with the Government. He drove a special kind of van called a 'security van'. Important and valuable things were transported in vans like these. Carl always drove to work the same way. He lived in a small village but worked in Bristol. There are a lot of Government offices in and near Bristol.

That morning Carl came round a bend and saw a dark green van in the middle of the road. There were two men there, too, outside the van. One of them waved to Carl. Carl stopped but didn't get out of his car. He rolled down his window.
'I wonder if you could help us. Something's wrong with the engine. Perhaps if you give us a push, it'll start again,' one of the men said. He was tall and wore round glasses. There was something strange about his eyes. Carl wasn't sure what it was. But he didn't think about it. He looked at his watch. He still had plenty of time before he had to be at work.
'All right. I'll be glad to help,' he said with a smile.
'Do you want me to give you a push with my car?' he asked.
'No, that won't be necessary. I mean, it'll be better if you and I just push it a bit with our hands. My friend can steer the van,' the other man said. He was tall, too. He wore dark glasses. They looked strange in the early morning light. It was still rather dark and the sun was covered with clouds.

Carl got out of his car. He and the man with dark glasses were behind the van. The other man got inside it, behind the steering wheel. Carl got ready to push. Then he felt something hard in his back. It was a gun and it belonged to the man with dark glasses.
'Get into the back! Fast! Or I'll use this,' he said. He opened the rear doors of the van. There was a third man there, behind them. Carl saw his face.
'It can't be. It's impossible,' he thought. Then everything went black when the man with dark glasses hit him over the head. He and the third man pushed and pulled Carl's body into the van. They shut the doors. Then the third man got out. He walked over to Carl's car and got in. The dark green van drove away. The third man drove away, too, in the direction of Bristol, where Carl worked. He looked just like Carl. He had the same face as Carl. But he wasn't Carl.

Questions.

1 What happened after Carl stopped?
2 Why was he so surprised when he saw the third man inside the van?
3 What do you think is going to happen now?

Unit Eleven

A

Good evening. We have three stories for you this evening in *The News in Focus*. Here are the headlines.

DIAMOND THIEVES ARRESTED IN NEW YORK
NEW HEART TRANSPLANT: PATIENT DOING WELL
BOMB FOUND NEAR SCHOOL

Five months ago two large diamonds were stolen from a shop in London. The diamonds were worth half a million pounds and were stolen by a man and a woman. Early this morning in New York the man and woman were arrested but the diamonds were not found. More about this story later in the programme.

1

England's latest heart-transplant patient, 45 year-old Mr Colin Kingston, is reported to be doing well in hospital this evening. Mr Kingston was given a new heart yesterday. The operation was carried out by a team of five surgeons in St Jude's hospital in London. A hospital spokesman says that Mr Kingston's chances 'are excellent!'

2

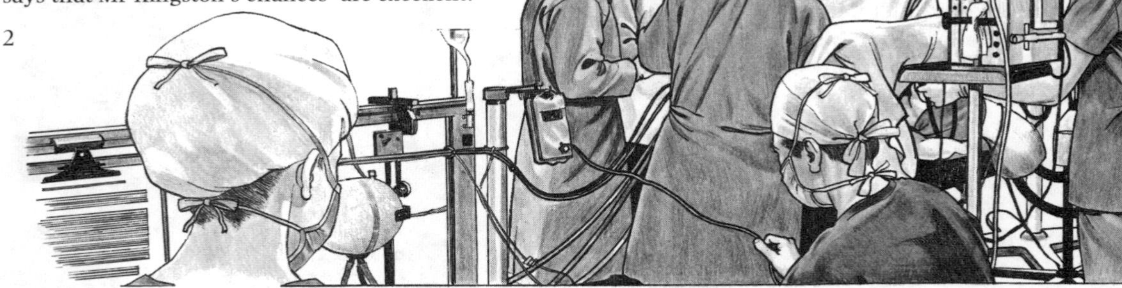

Two schoolchildren walked into a police station this afternoon and put a bomb on the table. They found it in a field near their school. It was later exploded by army experts. It was a small bomb but one of the experts later said, 'It's lucky the children weren't killed. The thing was still dangerous'. The bomb was probably dropped by a plane in World War II but never went off. It was more than 40 years old.

3

Answer.

1 Who do you think arrested the thieves?
2 What do you think a 'heart transplant' is?
3 Explain the third headline.

Picture one

1 Who stole the diamonds?
2 What happened to the man and woman this morning?
3 What about the diamonds?

Picture two

1 What happened to Mr Kingston yesterday?
2 Who did it?
3 How is Mr Kingston now?

Picture three

1 Ask and answer questions about the last story:
a Who ______________?
b Where ______________?
c When ______________?

B

1 Stop and look.

Sometimes you can tell from these examples what happened but not who did it. And sometimes you can tell both what happened and who did it.

1 The diamonds were stolen five months ago.
2 They were stolen by a man and a woman.
3 The man and woman were seen in New York.
4 They were seen by a detective.

All these sentences are examples of the *passive*. This form is used a lot in English, especially in the news (but also in everyday speech).
Notice that in examples 2 and 4, *by* is used to show who did it.

2 Ask questions beginning with *who* about these sentences. What are the answers?

Example: The diamonds were stolen by a man and a woman.
= Who stole the diamonds? – A man and a woman did.

1 The bomb was found by two schoolchildren.
2 It was later exploded by two army experts.
3 The man and woman were arrested by the police.
4 They were interviewed by a detective.
5 The operation was carried out by a team of surgeons.
6 The patient was later seen by his wife and daughter.

3 Re-write the sentences.

All these examples begin with *someone*. But we don't know who the *someone* is. Put them in the passive.

Example: Someone built this building in 1909.
= This building was built in 1909.

1 Someone found this money on the floor.
2 Someone killed the cat yesterday.
3 Someone stole the diamonds four months ago.
4 Someone dropped that bomb a long time ago.
5 Someone decorated this room last year.
6 Someone sent these letters here by mistake.

Unit Eleven

C

1 Listen to the dialogue.

The two schoolchildren who found the bomb are Simon and Pam. They live in a village and walk to school together. To get to school they have to cross some fields. They were on their way home from school when Simon saw something.

SIMON: Hey, look at that big hole over there!
PAM: It wasn't there this morning. I wonder what caused it.
SIMON: Probably the rain. Let's have a look.
PAM: Be careful! Don't fall in!
SIMON: It isn't very deep . . . hey, what do you think that is?
PAM: What?
SIMON: It looks like a . . . like a . . .
(*He goes down into the hole.*)
PAM: What are you doing? Don't go into the hole!
SIMON: I want to see what it is!
PAM: What? What are you talking about?
SIMON: This thing here!
(*He kicks it.*)
It's made of metal. Come down and look at it!
(*Pam comes down.*)
PAM: It may be a bomb. It may be dangerous.
SIMON: No! It's old. Look!
(*He kicks it again.*)
PAM: Don't do that . . . it may explode, or something.
SIMON: How do you think it got here?
PAM: I don't know. My dad says a lot of bombs were dropped here in the war.
SIMON: What do you think we should do with it?
PAM: Why don't we tell the police about it?
SIMON: Well, let's get it out of the hole first. Come on, help me lift it!
PAM: It's . . . it's heavier than it looks.
SIMON: Come on, it isn't that heavy. Why don't we carry it to the police station? Come on!

2 Answer.

1. Where did they find the bomb?
2. How did the bomb probably get there?
3. What does Pam think they should do?
4. What does Simon want to do?
5. What do you think they should do?
6. Why?

3 Find the phrase.

1. There is a phrase here that you can use when you think someone is doing something dangerous. What is it? Who says it? Where?
2. Think of some other situations when you could use this. For example: A child runs into the road. There are cars on the road. You shout ________!
3. There is also a phrase here that means *perhaps it is a* ________ . What is it? Who says it? Where?

Unit Eleven

D

1 Finding out what other people think.

What do you think that is? Do you think it's dangerous?
Where do you think it came from?
What do you think we should do with it?

Compare these questions with the more direct forms: *What is that? Is it dangerous? Where did it come from? What should we do with it?*

Ask these questions beginning *Do you think . . .? What do you think . . .? How do you think . . .?* etc.

1 Is it a bomb?
2 What kind of bomb is it?
3 Will it explode?
4 What can we do with it?
5 How can we get it out of the hole?
6 Should we leave it there?

2 Saying you aren't sure about something.

It may be a bomb. It may explode.

This is another use of *may*. Use it here to show you aren't sure about these things:

1 It will rain tomorrow.
2 I will come to your party a bit late.
3 This is wrong.
4 That man is a detective.
5 He has got a gun in his pocket.
6 He will kill you.

3 Making suggestions.

Let's tell the police. I think we should tell the police.
Why don't we tell the police?

In this situation, A and B's car has broken down. It is night and there is a town about 8 kilometres away. What are A and B saying?

A: Well, what do you think we ________ do now?
B: ________ leave the car here and walk into town.
A: Hmm. I think ________ ________ try to repair the engine.
B: It's too difficult. Why ________ ________ phone a garage and ask a mechanic to do it?
A: Look! Here comes a car.
B: All right. ________ stop it and ask him for a lift.
A: Good idea. ________ do that!

4 Listen to the dialogue on tape.

Unit Eleven

E

1 Find the two stories.

Here are two newspaper headlines. They are for two of the stories in *The News in Focus*.

A) INTERNATIONAL JEWEL THIEVES CAUGHT
B) MAN GIVEN NEW CHANCE OF LIFE

Now read each sentence (from 1 to 18). Say if the sentence belongs to headline A or headline B. Why do you think so?

1 Mr Colin Kingston became England's latest heart transplant patient today.
2 An English couple were arrested late last night in a hotel in New York.
3 Their names were not given to the press but it is believed they are Jennifer Watson and Martin Oakley.
4 He is 45 years old and has been in hospital since last May.
5 They are wanted by the police in at least five different countries.
6 Five months ago they stole two large diamonds from a shop in London.
7 Now at last he has a chance of leading a normal life again.
8 This was done in the middle of the day, in a busy street with thousands of people around.
9 But the couple were not stopped when they ran from the shop and jumped into a taxi.
10 The operation became possible when a 17 year-old boy was killed in a motorbike accident near Bristol over the weekend.
11 His parents gave their permission for his heart to be used in the operation.
12 Since then they have not been seen in England.
13 It was rushed to the hospital in London in a helicopter.
14 Doctors immediately began the operation.
15 'They have been here for about two weeks.'
16 'His chances are very good if he can get through the next 48 hours all right.'
17 'We think they probably wanted to do the same sort of thing here,' a police spokesman said in New York.
18 'But he is resting comfortably and we are all keeping our fingers crossed for him,' a doctor said after the operation.

2 Answer.

1 Describe what the English couple did five months ago.
2 What did the police in New York say about the couple?
3 Explain how Mr Kingston's operation became possible.
4 What did a doctor say about Mr Kingston?

3 Now tell someone else *one* of the stories!

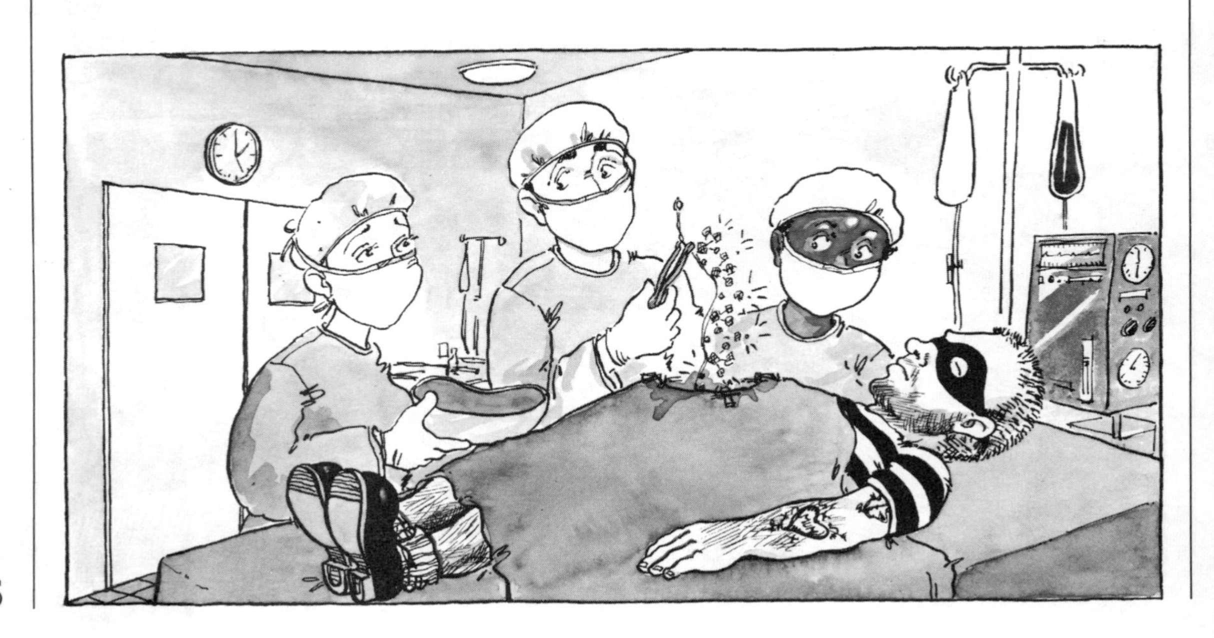

THE VISITOR

EPISODE ELEVEN

Questions.

1 What happened to Carl Eastwood in the last episode?
2 Read this episode and then answer these two questions:
a Who do you think 'Carl' really is?
b Why do you think this?

There was something strange about Carl that morning. Burt Harris didn't know what it was. Burt worked with Carl Eastwood. He was the guard in the security van which Carl drove. It was his job to stay in radio contact with the Government office they both worked for. There was a special two-way radio in all the vans. Burt could also contact the police on it.

They drove to the airport that morning. Carl didn't talk very much. That was strange, too. Carl usually talked a lot.
'Not very nice weather today,' Burt said. Carl didn't answer.

When they got to the airport, they went to a special office. There were men in uniform there. Valuable things were often sent to Bristol by air. Then they were taken from the office to places in and near Bristol. Burt showed one of the men some documents. Then two things were put in their van. One of them was a special sack with diamonds in it. The other thing was a small metal box. The box was locked but Burt knew there was microfilm in it. It came from a Government office in another part of England. The diamonds had to be taken to a bank in Bristol. But the metal box with the microfilm had to be taken to another Government office near the city.

They drove along the main road from the airport to the city centre. Every five minutes Burt told someone at the headquarters of the security company where they were. Carl said nothing. Then, a minute after one of Burt's radio reports, Carl suddenly turned off the main road.
'What are you doing that for?' Burt asked.
'I mean, why aren't you going straight to the bank?' Carl didn't answer. Suddenly Burt noticed something else. There was a light blue van behind them.
'I think that van is following us. It turned off when you did,' Burt said. He reached for the radio microphone. Carl stopped him.
'No, don't use the radio,' he said in a strange voice. Burt looked at him. He noticed his eyes. They never blinked.
'What are you talking about, Carl? You know what our orders are. I'm sure that van is . . .' He stopped and stared. Carl had a pistol in his hand. Carl stopped the security van. They were on a narrow road near a canal. The light blue van stopped behind them, too.
'What are you doing, Carl? What's happening?' They were Burt's last words. A second later he screamed. Carl shot him between the eyes.

The van was found twenty minutes later. Burt's body was there. So were the diamonds. But Carl and the metal box were gone.

Now think of some more questions you would like answers to, but which you can't find in this episode.

Unit Twelve

A

Our theme this week is *keeping fit*. This man isn't as fit as he used to be. Why not? What do you think?

Ten years ago I used to be very fit. I cycled to work and I got a lot of exercise at the weekends. I used to play tennis a lot and go for long walks. In those days I didn't earn very much. I had a job in an office. It wasn't a very good job but I had a lot of time to do the things I enjoyed doing.

Then, about eight years ago, I got a much better job. The pay was better. But the hours were a lot longer, too. I bought a car and drove to work every day. I began to take people out to lunch. 'Expense account' lunches. And I began to put on weight, too. I stopped playing tennis and going for long walks at the weekend because I just didn't have any time for things like that any more. There's a lot of stress in a job like mine. Perhaps that's why I started drinking more than I used to. For example, I used to have only a half a glass of whisky when I got home, then I started filling the glass to the top. Then I had another glass, and then another. I started smoking a lot, too. I never used to smoke at all.

Two months ago I had a heart attack. At first I just couldn't believe it. 'I'm too young,' I said. Luckily it wasn't very serious. I was in hospital a few days and they did a lot of tests. The doctor advised me to stop smoking and to eat less. He told me to do a lot of other things, too. But I don't see how I can do some of them and keep my job. For example, he advised me to work less, and get more exercise. But I just haven't any time! My job takes everything out of me!

Sometimes I wonder if I should get another job. Perhaps I could do something like I used to do. But if I do that, I won't earn as much. I have a family to support. I have to think of them, too. I just don't know what I should do. What do you think?

1 Answer.

1 What are some of the things this man *used to do* but which he doesn't do any more?
2 What are some of the things he probably enjoyed doing at the weekend?
3 Do you think he enjoys life as much as he used to? Give reasons for your answer.
4 What are the things he does now but which he didn't use to do?
5 What has his job to do with these things?
6 Do you think he should stop doing some things and start doing others? What? Why?

2 Role play.

Role A: You have a very difficult job. You smoke and drink a lot. You don't get any exercise. You are worried about your health. Go to a doctor for advice.

Role B: You are a doctor. Find out how much A smokes and drinks and how much exercise he/she gets. Then give some advice.

Unit Twelve

B

1 Stop and look.

I *used to* work in an office.
I *never used to* smoke very much,
I *used to* play tennis a lot.
I *used to* be a lot fitter than I am now.

This is a way of talking about things in the past which aren't true any more.

2 What about you?

Think of different times in your life. You probably did things then you don't do now.

1 When I was much younger, I used to be very interested in ________ .
2 A few years ago, I used to ________ but I don't any more.
3 When I was a baby, my mother tells me I used to ________ .
4 When I went to school I used to get up at ________ .

Think of some more examples!

3 What about this man?

Look at this man's trousers. Are those the trousers he used to wear? Or are they the trousers he usually wears now? He used to do a lot of things he doesn't do any more. And on the other hand he never used to do things he does now. Make full sentences.

He used to ________ .
He never used to ________ .

1 a lot of beer
2 four big meals every day
3 any exercise
4 tennis
5 very fat

4 What do you think?

How should these three people get fit? Think of some good ways. Think of some bad ways, too.

Ken Chapton, 43, language school director. Smokes 15 cigars a day, always very busy, drives everywhere in his car.

Monica Vance, 52, housewife. Works in the garden a lot. She often gets a very bad pain in her back. Overweight, doesn't sleep well, very nervous.

Leonard Kale, 21, student, smokes 5 cigarettes a day, has a lot of time but never gets any fresh air. Very thin (he thinks that's why women don't like him).

Unit Twelve

C

1 Listen to the dialogue.

Mrs Vance has gone to see a doctor about the pain in her back.

DR KEAN: Now, Mrs Vance. What's the problem?
MONICA: It's my back. I have a terrible pain down here. Can you see?
DR KEAN: Hmm. How long have you had it?
MONICA: For two weeks now. And it's getting worse.
DR KEAN: Have you had this trouble before?
MONICA: Yes, I have. But it's never been this bad before.
DR KEAN: Do you think you can lie down on this couch . . . on your back?
MONICA: I don't know . . . I . . . I'll try.
(*Lies down.*)
Oh . . .
DR KEAN: Does your back hurt now?
MONICA: Yes, it does.
DR KEAN: Hmm. Now . . . I'd like you to lift your right leg as high as you can. Can you try, please?
MONICA: (*Groans.*)
I can't get it any higher than that.
DR KEAN: And now the other one, please.
MONICA: (*Groans again.*)
Like this?
DR KEAN: Can you get it any higher?
MONICA: No, I can't. I . . . I . . . no, I can't. It hurts a lot when I do that.
(*A few minutes later.*)
DR KEAN: Now, first I'll give you a prescription.
MONICA: Is it something for the pain?
DR KEAN: Yes, I think it'll stop it. But I'm also going to arrange an appointment for you at the hospital.
MONICA: Hospital? Oh! Do I have to go to hospital?
DR KEAN: Yes, but only for some X-rays. Now . . . here's the prescription. Just take it to any chemist's. And the nurse will make the appointment at the hospital for you when you go out.
MONICA: Thank you very much, doctor.

2 Explain the picture.

Listen to the dialogue. Then explain what is happening in the picture. What do you think Mrs Vance and the doctor are saying?

3 Answer.

1 What does Mrs Vance tell the doctor about the pain?
2 What does he ask her to do?
3 What does he give her?
4 What else is going to happen?

4 Role play.

You have a pain in your stomach. It started three days ago and it is getting worse. You get it after you eat. You see a doctor about it. He gives you a prescription and sends you to hospital for some 'simple tests'. Work out the dialogue.

Unit Twelve

1 Listen to Laura's story.

Here is one person who really believes in keeping fit. Her name is Mrs Laura Taylor. She is 45 but looks at least 10 years younger. Let's listen to her story.

It all started about two years ago. In those days things were very different. I was overweight. I used to smoke a lot – about 30 cigarettes a day. I never got any exercise. I used to stay at home all day. I never went out into the fresh air, except to do the shopping. And even then I used to take the car. One day I looked at myself in the mirror.

'My God,' I thought. 'I look terrible!' I tried to touch my toes. I couldn't do it. I found an old dress. I couldn't put it on. It was too small. Or rather, I was too fat!

The next day I tried to jog a little. At first it was terrible. I mean, I just couldn't run. Not even a short distance. And at first people used to laugh at me.

'Why are you running? Are you in a hurry?' they shouted.

But now I've completely changed the way I live. I've stopped eating meat and I've started eating far more fresh vegetables. My husband and daughter have started that, too. At first they didn't like the new food. But they've changed. About six months ago I sold my car and bought a bike. Recently I've started doing yoga exercises. My husband often goes cycling with me now and my daughter jogs with me in the evening. They've both lost weight and are much healthier than they used to be, too.

2 Questions.

1 Describe the way Laura Taylor used to live.
2 Describe what happened one day about two years ago.
3 Describe the things she and her family have started doing in the last two years.

Unit Twelve

E

1 Stop and look.

Look at the first, second, etc. sentences in each box. Notice how the tense form changes.

No definite time
Have you had the trouble before?
Have you seen a doctor about it?
Mrs Taylor has sold her car.
She has bought a bike.
She has started doing yoga exercises.

Definite time in the past
Yes, I had it last year.
Yes, I saw one a few days ago.
She sold it six months ago.
She bought it six months ago, too.
She started doing them a few months ago.

We often use the present perfect tense to talk about past things but only when we do not mention a definite past time.
When you mention a definite time in the past, you have to use the past simple tense.

2 Look at the question and finish the answer.

1 Have you seen this film before? – Yes, I ________ it last Friday.
2 Have you been to America? – Yes, I ________ there last year.
3 Have you ever had a Chinese meal? – Yes, I ________ one a few weeks ago.
4 Have you done your homework? – Yes, I ________ it last night.

3 Study the two different question forms.

Monica has had the trouble before.
Has Monica had the trouble before?

She had it last year.
Did she have it last year?

Ask questions about Mrs Taylor:

Example: Ask if she has sold her car.
= Has she sold her car?
Ask when she sold it.
= When did she sell it?

Now ask:
1 if she has lost weight.
2 how much she lost last month.
3 if she has started yoga exercises.
4 when she started them.
5 if her husband has lost weight, too.
6 if her daughter has jogged with her.
7 when she jogged with her.
8 if her husband lost any weight last month.

WHAT PEOPLE SAY

Now turn to page 105 and listen to the tape to find out what people say about keeping fit.

THE VISITOR

EPISODE TWELVE

Questions.

1 Who was Carl Eastwood?
2 What happened to him?
3 Which of these do you think is correct? Explain why.
a The man who looked like Carl wasn't really him at all.
b Carl was really a dangerous criminal all the time but nobody knew that.

The helicopter landed on the deck of the large, light blue yacht. A man in grey got out. He was smiling. He went to a cabin below the deck. Shandor was waiting there for him. He looked at him with his cold, blue eyes.
'Well, Harlan? Did you follow my instructions?'
'Yes, Mr Shandor. Here is the microfilm. I think it will tell you everything you want to know.' Shandor took the microfilm and put it into a small machine. The machine made the things on the microfilm larger and projected them onto a small screen. Shandor studied the film carefully.
'Yes, it's all here. Plans for some of the weapons we didn't know about before,' he said. He looked at Harlan again.
'And what about my other instructions?'
'Eastwood's body was thrown into the sea. It will never be found. The police think he was really a criminal or a spy. They'll never know the truth,' Harlan answered.

For the first time Shandor smiled.
'No, they won't. They could never believe the truth. Never!' He looked very satisfied. Harlan stepped closer to Shandor's desk.
'There's still some unfinished business with the young journalist. I wonder if we could talk about that now?' Shandor didn't answer. Harlan went on.
'After his little . . . er . . . accident . . . he was taken to hospital. He's still there. Do you think something should be done about him?' Shandor smiled again. It was a cold smile.
'Mr Redford probably knows far too much about us. What do you suggest, Harlan? Have you got some sort of plan?'
'Yes, Mr Shandor, I have! We have another operator ready. This one looks just like Redford's boss. I suggest that our operator should visit Mr Redford in hospital. The operator will give him a little gift. Some chocolate. Some very special chocolate. And Redford will eat it. All of it. Our operator will make sure of that.'

Shandor thought for a moment.
'Yes, I think I know the kind of chocolate you mean. An excellent idea!' he said. Both men smiled coldly.

Question.

What do you think the 'operator' is going to do?

Unit Thirteen

A

Hello. In this evening's *The News in Focus* we look at only one story.

In the village of Helmby, in the north of England, there was a demonstration today. The demonstration became a riot. Some people were hurt. Others were arrested. Our reporter, Ian Keys, has been in the village all day:

This is what the trouble was all about. The plan to build an atomic power station here. If the government builds it, it will be one of the largest in Europe. It will produce enough energy for three cities the size of Manchester.

But not everybody agrees with the plan. Early this morning a large group of people gathered to demonstrate against it. They marched slowly through the village in the heavy rain. At first everything was calm. The police watched quietly.

But then some of the demonstrators tried to march into a field where work on the first part of the station had just begun. The police stopped them. Fighting began. Stones were thrown. When the trouble began, more police came quickly. Arrests were made. The police pushed the demonstrators back into the village. Shop windows were smashed. More arrests were made.

Now, at the end of the day, at least 50 demonstrators have been arrested. Several policemen were badly hurt in the fighting and are now in hospital. But things are quiet and calm in the village again. It is still raining heavily.

Answer.

1 What happened today in Helmby?
2 What exactly is Helmby?
3 What does the government plan to do there?
4 How much energy will it produce?
5 Who gathered together?
6 Why?
7 What did they do?
8 Describe how the trouble started.
9 What was thrown?
10 What happened after they were thrown?
11 What did the police do?
12 What are things like now?

Unit Thirteen

B

1 Stop and look.

> The group marched *slowly* through the village.
> When the trouble began, the police came *quickly*.
> Things are *quiet* and *calm* again.

Words like *quiet, calm, slow, bad,* etc. are *adjectives.* We use them with *nouns.* What are the nouns in the following examples? What are the adjectives?

The demonstration was quiet and calm.
He gave a bad speech.
The rain was heavy.
She is a very good dancer.

Slowly and *quickly* are *adverbs.* Adverbs are used to describe how people do things or how things happen. What are the adverbs here? Why do we use them in these examples?

The demonstration began quietly and calmly.
He spoke badly.
It rained heavily.
She dances very well.

2 Look at these sentences. Which form of the word goes in which sentence?

Example: (*slow/slowly*) Speak ________, please.
= Speak slowly, please.
This train is very ________.
= This train is very slow.

1 (*quiet/quietly*)
a Please be ________ when you are in the hospital.
b He always speaks very ________.

2 (*quick/quickly*)
a Please come ________.
b This is a ________ way to lose weight.

3 (*clear/clearly*)
a You don't write very ________.
b Your writing isn't very ________.

4 (*good/well*)
a I'm not a very ________ swimmer.
b I don't dance very ________.

5 (*free/freely*)
a You can speak ________.
b Excuse me. Are these seats ________?

6 (*dangerous/dangerously*)
a He drove very ________.
b Atomic power is ________.

Unit Thirteen

C

1 Listen to the dialogue.

Later, Ian Keys spoke to two people in the village. One of them, Dave, is a schoolteacher. The other, Christine, works in a factory near the village. They met in a local pub.

IAN: What do you think of the plan to build the atomic power station here?

CHRISTINE: Well . . . I don't see what else we can do. I mean, it has to be built somewhere. Everybody knows we need atomic power.

DAVE: I . . . I don't agree at all. It will ruin the village. And in any case I don't think it *is* necessary. In fact I think it's unnecessary and unsafe.

CHRISTINE: What do you mean it's unnecessary? Everybody knows we can't go on using oil much longer. In 20 or 30 years . . . perhaps sooner . . . there won't be any. And look at what it costs already.

DAVE: Well . . . first of all, that simply isn't true. I mean, nobody knows how much oil is left. But even if it runs out in 20 or 30 years there'll be alternative sources of energy.

CHRISTINE: What do you mean? How do you think we're going to heat our homes and light them, and run our factories when the oil runs out? What do you think we're going to use then? Old socks? Because that'll be the only . . . what do you call it . . . alternative source of energy there'll be!

DAVE: I'm sorry, but that's nonsense. Just nonsense!

CHRISTINE: No, it isn't. I don't see how you can say . . .

DAVE: My God, think of all the coal down there in the mines. Nobody really knows how much there is but there's enough for the next 200 years at least!

CHRISTINE: Don't talk to me about the coal mines! My father worked in them all his life! And when he died last year, his lungs were hard as stone. He used to cough up blood! I don't think anybody should work in a coal mine.

DAVE: There are better ways of digging up coal than sending men down into the mines. And anyway, that's only one of the possibilities. In a few years we'll be able to use the sun . . . and the wind . . .

CHRISTINE: That's a load of old rubbish! Anyway, if we build the station here, it will bring a lot of jobs to the area. And that's what we really need here. Jobs!

DAVE: Atomic power stations don't bring many jobs with them.

CHRISTINE: Yes, they do!

DAVE: No, they don't!

2 Answer.

1 Who is for the plan?
2 Who is against it?
3 Give at least one reason why one of the people is for the plan.
4 Give at least one reason why the other person is against it.

3 What exactly do these words mean?

1 '*It* will ruin the village.'
2 'And look at what *it* costs already.'
3 '*That* simply isn't true.'
4 '*That'll* be the only alternative source of energy there'll be!'
5 '*That's* nonsense.'
6 '*That's* a load of old rubbish!'

Unit Thirteen

D

1 After *when* or *if*, use the present simple.

If we *build* the station here, it will ruin the village.
What will we do when there'*s* no more oil?
Even if it *runs* out, there'll be alternative sources of energy!
If we *build* the station here, it will bring jobs to the area.

2 Find a word to finish these sentences.

1 (*student on a bus*) Will you please tell me when we ________ to the language school?
2 (*letter from one friend to another*) Will you be at the airport when I ________?
3 (*patient to doctor*) Will the pain go away if I ________ this medicine?
4 (*boss to secretary*) If you ________ that mistake again, I'll sack you!
5 (*friend to friend*) Come to the party. I'm sure you'll enjoy it if you ________.
6 (*mother to child*) You can go out when the rain ________.

3 Agreeing and disagreeing.

Look at these ways of agreeing and disagreeing. Which are the strongest forms? Which are the most polite?

Nonsense!/I don't quite agree./How can you say that?/What a load of rubbish!
I think so, too./I agree entirely./That's exactly what I think!

Agree or disagree with these statements:
1 Any idiot can learn English in a few hours.
2 It takes a long time to learn English well.
3 Women shouldn't work. They should stay at home.
4 Everybody knows that English cooking is the best in the world.
5 It may not be the best but it isn't as bad as people say it is.
6 Men and women should be equal but they aren't.

Think of some more statements you agree or disagree with.

4 Open dialogue.

Christine and Dave are still arguing. Finish their sentences.

CHRISTINE: We need jobs here.
DAVE: Yes, I __(1)__ with that, but that doesn't __(2)__ we need an atomic power station.
CHRISTINE: I __(3)__ ________ at all! I __(4)__ it's the only way we can get jobs here.
DAVE: How __(5)__ you __(6)__ that? There are other industries.
CHRISTINE: No other __(7)__ wants to start a factory here.
DAVE: __(8)__ !
CHRISTINE: No, it __(9)__ !
DAVE: Yes, it __(10)__ !
CHRISTINE: What a __(11)__ of rubbish!

Where do these words belong?
a) is b) can c) isn't d) say e) load f) industry g) Nonsense h) agree i) don't agree j) think k) mean

5 You can listen to the dialogue on tape.

Unit Thirteen

E

1 Nuclear power: for and against.

Nuclear power seems in some ways much cleaner than other sources of energy. Take oil or coal as an example. When they are used in power stations, a great deal of smoke is produced. The smoke contains a great deal of acid. Even if the smoke is cleaned by filters, a lot of the acid still escapes into the air. This can be carried by clouds from power stations in England to Scandinavia. When it rains there, the acid comes down with the rain. As a result, the fish in lakes and trees in forests begin to die.

But many people are still against nuclear power. They believe that the problem is not just the danger of an accident in the atomic power station. Highly radioactive material is used. Radioactivity can cause cancer and other illnesses. Only a part of the material is used. The rest – called waste – is just as radioactive. Although it is still highly dangerous, this radioactive waste is often thrown into the sea. Nobody can be certain what will happen to it there. Only one thing is certain. It will be highly dangerous for at least 240,000 years!

Another problem was shown in the film *The China Syndrome*. What if there is an explosion in the nuclear reactor (the part that produces the nuclear energy)? If one explodes near a large city, how many people will die? Other experts argue that this is impossible. But the argument will go on for a long time. And it is also clear that nuclear power can never be the only answer. It is only one possible answer. Some other possibilities are solar power (from the sun), wind power and tidal power (from the waves and tides in the ocean). And we must conserve energy, too. Conservation will become more and more of a necessity.

2 Answer.

1 Explain how smoke from power stations in England can kill fish and trees in Scandinavia.
2 Explain what happens to radioactive waste and how it can be a problem.
3 What problem was shown in *The China Syndrome?*
4 What are some of the other possible sources of energy?

3 Word study.

Use the word in another form.

Example: (*cloud*) It's ________ today.
=It's cloudy today.

1 (*danger*) Do you think nuclear power is ________?
2 (*radioactive*) Is ________ a big problem?
3 (*contain*) What happens to the waste after it is put into ________?
4 (*explode*) Could there be an ________?
5 (*possible*) Is that a ________?
6 (*argue*) What's your ________ for nuclear power?

THE VISITOR

EPISODE THIRTEEN

Revision questions.

1. Tony Redford is in hospital. Why?
2. Do you think he is in any danger there? Give reasons for your answer.
3. Re-tell some of the other important things that have happened in the story so far.

Tony looked around his hospital room unhappily. It was his second day there. It was a big room and he was all alone in it. The door opened and Liz Davis came in.
'Liz! Thank God you've come! When are they going to let me out of here?' he asked loudly.
'When they know you're all right. They have to examine you very carefully. All sorts of things happen to people who have accidents like yours,' she answered.
'But Liz, I tell you it wasn't an accident! I was pushed in front of that train. I don't know who did it because I didn't see him. But I was pushed!' Tony wanted to say more but he could see that his boss didn't really believe him. He wondered where Tan-Lin was.
'I hope she comes soon. She'll understand what I'm talking about,' he thought. Suddenly he noticed something strange about Liz. She had a yellow dress on.
'I've never seen you in a yellow dress before, Liz. I thought you didn't like yellow,' he said. The colour went very badly with her red hair. Liz didn't answer.
'Is that a new dress you're wearing?' he asked more loudly. But she still didn't answer. She had a box in her hands. She began to unwrap it.
'I've brought you a gift. I hope you'll like it, Tony,' she said slowly. Tony stared at the box. It was a box of chocolates. But Tony hated chocolates. He never ate them. And Liz knew that very well. For a moment he wondered if it was some kind of joke. But it wasn't.
'Here. Have one. You'll feel much better if you do. Chocolate gives you energy, you know. It's good for you!' she said. Tony stared at her. She came closer with the chocolate.
'Well, er . . . thanks a lot, Liz, but I'll eat them later if you don't mind,' he answered. But she shook her head.
'No, Tony. You must eat them now.'
'But I'm not really very hungry, Liz!' She stared at him strangely.
'It's good for you!' she repeated slowly. She spoke almost like a parrot.
She tried to push the chocolate into his mouth.
'No, Liz. I don't want it,' Tony said. He could taste some of the chocolate on his lips. And the taste wasn't sweet at all but bitter.

Suddenly Liz gripped him. It was a grip of steel! She forced him down in the bed and stood over him with the chocolate.
'I disagree, Tony. You want this chocolate. And you will eat it. And all the other chocolates in the box. You will eat the chocolate now! Quickly!' Tony looked into Liz's eyes. There was a cold, terrible look in them.
'My God, perhaps I'm dreaming. Perhaps it's all a terrible nightmare,' he thought.

Question.

What do you think Liz is trying to do?

Unit Fourteen

A

This is Claire Walton with *Theme of the Week* again. And our theme this week is *fear and hope*.

What are some of the things you are afraid will happen? And what do you hope will happen? Here are some of the answers from four different people.

Eileen Chase, tax expert
I'm afraid of dogs. I was bitten once when I was a child. So when I see one now, I'm afraid it will bite me. I often have a nightmare. In it a huge dog with sharp teeth runs after me. I run very fast, but it runs much faster. I can hear it behind me. I hope it won't catch me, but it does. I wake up screaming.

1

Barney Thomas, tramp and street musician
I don't think I'm afraid of anything. Not really. Well, hmm, let me see . . . perhaps I'm afraid it'll rain tonight and I'll get wet. I'll probably sleep on a park bench tonight. I hope I'll find a comfortable one . . . I live from day to day. That's why I never worry about anything.

2

Lorraine Taylor, student
I have to take my final exams soon, and naturally I'm a bit worried about them. I hope I'll pass them. My parents will be very disappointed if I don't . . . if I fail them, I mean. I have to study very hard. I hope I'll get a good result. It's very important. I've just got to pass them! I've just got to!

3

Charles L. Night, poet
There's only one thing I'm really afraid of. Another big war! I was in the last one. I hope something like that never happens again. I'm afraid the next one will be much worse. If it happens, that is. But I hope it won't! I really do!

4

Unit Fourteen

B

Answer.

Picture one

1 How does Eileen Chase feel about dogs?
2 Why?
3 Describe her nightmare.

Picture two

1 Would you like to be Barney Thomas tonight? Give reasons.
2 Think of some things he is probably afraid will happen but which he *doesn't* mention.
3 Describe some of the things he probably hopes will happen in the next few days.

Picture three

1 Why do you think Lorraine is so worried about her exams?
2 What do you think she is going to do almost every evening this week?
3 Why is she going to do this?

Picture four

1 Talk about what Charles Night is afraid of and why.

Now talk about some of the things you hope and fear.

1 Talking about fear and hope.

These two women are running a race. They're both in front but two other runners are close behind them. What do you think these two hope will happen? What are they afraid will happen?

See if you can finish these sentences about the two runners:

1 Number five hopes she ________ ________ the race.
2 In other words, she hopes she ________ get to the finish before number three.
3 But she is afraid number three ________ ________ there before she does.
4 They are both afraid that the other runners ________ catch up with them.
5 Naturally, she hopes this ________ happen. That's why they're running so fast.

2 Two irregular adverbs.

In the nightmare, I run *very* fast. I have to study very *hard* for my exams.

In Unit 13, you studied some *adverbs*:
The rain was heavy. = It rained very *heavily*.
She is a good dancer. = She dances *well*.

But *fast* and *hard* don't change like that:
I'm a fast runner. = I can run very *fast*.
I'm a hard worker. = I work very *hard*.

Make your own examples. Sometimes you have to change the form. Sometimes you don't.

1 Bill's a dangerous driver. = He drives ________.
2 Mary's a fast driver. = She drives ________.
3 I'm not a good speaker. = I don't speak very ________.
4 Your writing isn't clear. = You don't write very ________.
5 I did a lot of hard work yesterday. = I had to work ________.
6 I'm a bad singer. = I ________ very ________.

Unit Fourteen

C

1 Read the story.

A lot of our fears are about money. For example, are you ever afraid you'll get a bill some day, and won't be able to pay it? This newspaper article is about a man who was very afraid of things like that.

Computer error: man almost drops dead

Mr Arthur Henderson, 45, of Redhill, Surrey, is a very careful man. He is especially careful about electricity. He never uses very much and his bill, which he pays every three months, is usually around £25. Last week, however, Mr Henderson had a very nasty surprise. When his latest electricity bill arrived, it was for £259.00. Over ten times as much.

'I can't see very well without my glasses, and at first I couldn't find them anywhere. When I finally did and had a good look at the bill, I almost had a heart attack. It began to beat very fast. I felt terrible,' Mr Henderson said.

Luckily his sister, Betty, lives nearby and came to see him a few minutes later.

'He was very upset when I got there. Very upset. He was looking at the bill and shaking his head. I calmed him down and made him a cup of tea. Then I offered to ring the Electricity Board for him,' she told a reporter.

As a result of her phone call, Mr Henderson got a corrected bill from the Electricity Board a few days later. He also got a note of apology.

'I was very glad when I got it,' Mr Henderson said. 'It seems the new computer made a mistake. It put a decimal point in the wrong place and added a "0". The corrected bill was £25.90, not £259.00.'

2 Ask and answer.

1 How much does Mr Henderson usually ________ ?
2 Why was he so worried when ________ ?
3 Who ________ ?
4 What did she ________ ?
5 What happened after ________ ?

3 Look at the three pictures.

1 What is happening in them?
2 What has just happened?
3 What is going to happen next?
4 Imagine the dialogue in pictures two and three.

1

2

3

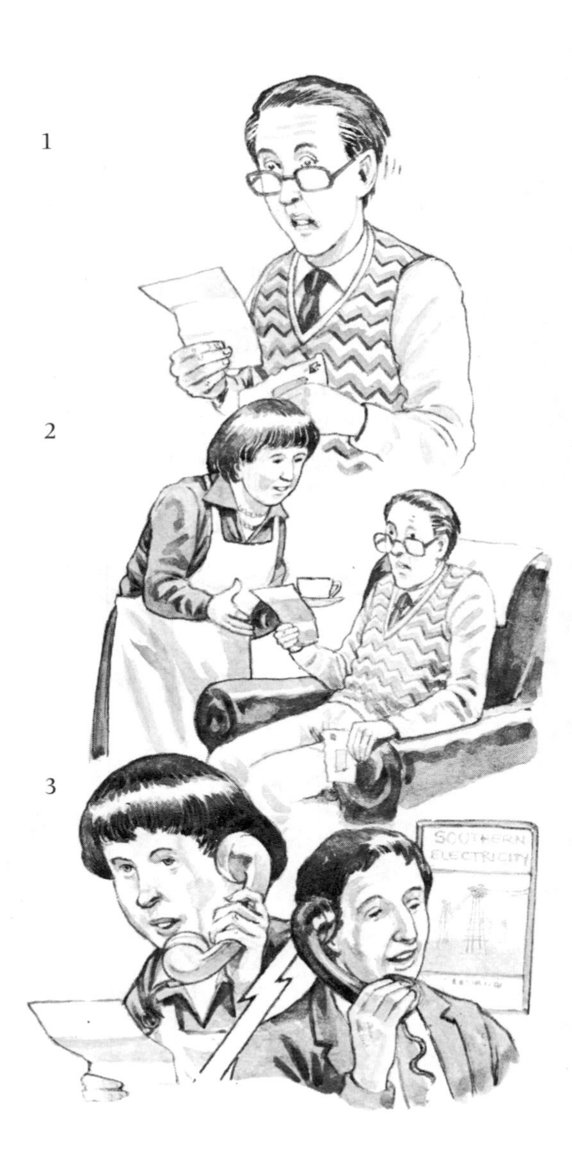

Unit Fourteen

1 Find the dialogue.

Read Betty's part on the left. Get someone else to read Arthur's part on the right.

1 You look terrible! What is it?
2 Let me see it, Arthur.
3 Hmm. This is far too high. There's clearly some kind of mistake.
4 Even if you did, it's still far too high! Shall I phone the Electricity Board about it?
5 Let me find it for you, Arthur. Ah, here it is. Would you like me to phone now?
6 No, let me do it, Arthur. You're far too upset.

a I'm not so sure. I mean, perhaps it's right. Perhaps I left the water heater on, or something.
b Hmm, that's a good idea. The number's here in this book somewhere.
c Perhaps you're right. I think I'll just sit down for a moment.
d Here you are. Have a look at it.
e This electricity bill has just come and it's ten times higher than usual.
f No, now that I've got the number, I can do it.

2 Now listen to the dialogue at least once on tape.

3 What do the words in italics mean?

1 You look terrible. What is *it*?
2 Let me see *it*, Arthur.
3 Even if you *did*, it's still far too high!
4 Let me do *it*, Arthur. You're far too upset.

4 Role play.

Role A: You are Arthur's friend. You are phoning the Electricity Board. Tell them about Arthur's bill and how much he usually pays. You are sure it is a mistake. Get them to check it again.

Role B: You work for the Electricity Board. Listen politely to what Arthur's friend says. Ask if it is possible that Arthur has left a water heater on or something. Then promise to 'look into the matter as soon as possible'.

Unit Fourteen

E

1 Would you like me to ________?

Finish the dialogue in the three situations.

OLD MAN: Oh, this suitcase is heavy!
YOUNG WOMAN: Would you like ________ to ________ it for you?
OLD MAN: Oh, that's very kind of you.

MAN: I have to be at the airport before 11.30.
CLERK: ________ you like ________ to phone for a taxi ________ you, sir?
MAN: Yes, please.

A: Oh, my God. I forgot to go to the bank today. I need £50.
B: ________ you ________ ________ to lend you the money?
A: Could you?

2 Let me do it!

Study this dialogue.

BETTY: Would you like me to phone the Electricity Board for you?
ARTHUR: No, no. I'll do it. I . . . I . . .
BETTY: No, let me phone them for you! You're too upset.

Finish Betty's part in the three dialogues.

1
BETTY: ________ you like me to make you a cup of tea?
ARTHUR: No, I'll make one.
BETTY: No, ________ me ________ it for you!

2
BETTY: Would ________ ________ ________ to pay the bill?
ARTHUR: No, I can pay it.
BETTY: No, ________ ________ ________ ________ . You haven't got enough money.

3
BETTY: ________ ________ ________ ________ to write a letter to the Electricity Board?
ARTHUR: No, I'll write it.
BETTY: No, ________ ________ ________ it!

3 Shall I phone them for you?

When you offer to do something, it is also possible to say this:

ARTHUR: I think I'll phone the Electricity Board.
BETTY: *Shall I phone* them for you?
ARTHUR: Oh . . . that's very kind of you. Do you mind?

In the same way, offer to do these things:

1 carry an old man's suitcase
2 phone a taxi for a friend
3 lend a friend some money
4 make a cup of tea
5 explain the word *upset*
6 close the window

THE VISITOR

EPISODE FOURTEEN

Tony is in hospital and his boss, Liz Davis, is trying to force chocolate down his throat. Why do you think she is doing this?

'I hope you won't give me any trouble with the chocolate! What are you afraid of?' Liz said. She was holding him down with only one hand. She had the strength of a tiger. Tony looked up into her eyes and felt more and more afraid. In fact he was terrified. There was no feeling in those eyes. They were cold and they never blinked. He opened his mouth and tried to scream. But she forced her hand into his mouth and stopped him. He tried to bite that hand, but it was impossible. It was like trying to bite a lump of steel. Suddenly, with a sick feeling in his stomach, Tony realised that this thing with Liz's face and voice wasn't really Liz at all. It was some kind of terrible machine that looked like a human being but wasn't.
'Would you like me to help you? I mean, shall I help you to eat this nice chocolate?' the thing with Liz's face asked. It held him down with its knee and forced open Tony's mouth with one of its hands. With the other it forced a big piece of the bitter chocolate into his mouth. And Tony was sure it wasn't chocolate at all but some kind of poison. Tony spat it out. The thing with Liz's face began to force another piece into his mouth. Tony knew he was losing his strength. He was getting weaker and weaker.
But suddenly he saw another face in the room. It was Tan-Lin. The short, red-haired machine with the strength of a tiger turned around very fast, and faced the tall, thin woman. For a moment neither of them moved. Then the machine cut through the air with its hand. That hand was like a knife, but Tan-Lin moved very fast, too. Somehow she moved away. The machine kicked out at her with one leg. But Tan-Lin moved away from the kick, too. The machine was fast but Tan-Lin was faster. She chopped at its neck, like a karate expert. The machine with Liz's face stopped, but only for a moment. It cut through the air again with its knife-like hand, and Tan-Lin again moved away from the blow. She chopped a second time at the same place on the machine's neck. This time a kind of blue spark came from one of the thing's eyes.
Tan-Lin moved in quickly and chopped a third time at exactly the same place. There were more blue sparks. The thing that looked and spoke like Liz suddenly froze. It stood there but didn't move. Its eyes stared out lifelessly. One of its hands was still in the air, like a frozen karate fighter.
'I think I came just in time, don't you agree, Mr Redford?' Tan-Lin said softly.

Questions.

1. Do you agree that the thing with Liz's face is some kind of machine? Give reasons.
2. Who do you think made the machine?

Unit Fifteen

A

Hello again. This evening in *The News in Focus* we'll be looking at three stories behind the headlines.

MOUNTAIN RESCUE DRAMA
BOY PREVENTS TRAIN DISASTER
POP STAR WINS OSCAR

1

At about three o'clock yesterday afternoon, a young man and woman were climbing a mountain in Scotland. The sun was shining and the sky was clear, but the young woman thought a storm was coming. She wanted to turn back but her companion didn't. She tried to persuade him to come with her. He refused and went on alone. The storm came and he was trapped on the mountain all night. This morning he was rescued by helicopter and taken to hospital. We'll learn more about this story later in the programme.

2

Only a few hours later, at six o'clock, the London to Brighton express was coming out of a tunnel when the driver saw a boy on the line in front of him. The boy was waving his arms and shouting. Why? What was he doing there? And how did the boy prevent a terrible disaster and save a great many lives? More about this story later in the programme, too.

3

Yesterday evening in Hollywood, a very important ceremony took place. This year's 'Oscars' were awarded. One of the biggest surprises was the prize for this year's best actress. It went to Judy Garrett for her new serious film, *The Bridge*. Judy wasn't even at the ceremony. She was watching television at home when she heard the news. And when she heard it, she fainted.

'I never thought I had a chance. That's why I didn't go to the ceremony,' Judy said later.

Answer.

Picture one

1 Why did the young woman want to turn back?
2 What did the young man want to do?
3 What are some of the things you think the woman said? Think of her exact words!
4 And what do you think the young man said?

Picture two

1 The train driver was very surprised. Why?
2 But later he was glad he saw the boy. Why?
3 Why do you think the boy was waving his arms and shouting?

Picture three

1 What is an 'Oscar'? How often are they awarded?
2 Why was Judy so surprised?
3 What was she doing when she heard the news?
4 What happened when she heard it?

1 Stop and look.

> When I got up this morning, the sun *was shining*.
> But when I looked out of the window at ten o'clock, it *was raining*.

'The sun was shining' and 'It was raining' are examples of the *past progressive*. We use this form when we talk about something which wasn't finished in the past. For instance, in the first example, the sun started to shine before I got up. Do you think it started to rain before I looked out of the window? Find other examples of this past form in the news stories.

2 Look at the two pictures. Then answer the questions.

1 What was the man doing when the phone rang?
2 What did he do when it rang?
3 Choose the correct form; a, b or c.
The man ________ a letter when his wife ________ him.

a writes	a phones
b was writing	b was phoning
c wrote	c phoned

3 Use a form of the verb in brackets to finish this story.

1 At seven o'clock yesterday evening I (*listen*) the radio.
2 Outside it (*rain*) very hard.
3 Suddenly I (*hear*) a knock at the door.
4 I (*get*) up and (*open*) the door.
5 My friend (*stand*) there. He (*have*) his dog with him.
6 'I (*take*) my dog for a walk when this rain (*start*),' he said.

Unit Fifteen

C

1 Listen to the dialogue.

A young man and woman, David and June, are climbing a mountain in Scotland. They have stopped for a minute.

JUNE: Hmm. Look at the sky. Do you think there's going to be a storm?
DAVID: I doubt it. Look! The sun's shining.
JUNE: But look at those clouds.
DAVID: They're a long way away. Nothing to worry about.
JUNE: But the weather here can change very quickly.
DAVID: There's nothing to worry about, I tell you. Come on. We're wasting time.
JUNE: I don't agree. I mean, those clouds are . . .
DAVID: Don't worry about them. It may rain a little, that's all. Are you afraid of getting wet?

JUNE: No, I'm not. But I don't want to get caught up here in a really bad storm.
DAVID: Storm? What storm? There isn't going to be a storm, I tell you. Now let's start climbing again.
JUNE: I don't think that's a good idea. I really don't.
DAVID: Look, are you coming with me or aren't you?
(Suddenly there is an echo of thunder in the distance.)
JUNE: Listen! Thunder!
DAVID: So what? Come on. Let's go.
JUNE: I don't think we should go on. I really don't!
DAVID: Well, I do! I'm going to the top!
JUNE: Well, I'm not! I'm turning back.
DAVID: All right! I'll go on alone!
JUNE: Don't be a fool, David. Come back with me.
(There is more thunder, and a flash of lightning.)
David! Come back! Listen to me, David!
(The wind begins to blow hard.)

2 Answer.

1 Why is June worried?
2 What does David want to do?
3 What does June want to do?
4 What do you think they should do? Why?

3 Think and find.

1 Find some of the phrases David uses to try to persuade June to go on with him.
2 Now find the phrases that June uses to persuade him *not* to go on.

4 Role play.

You and your friend are in a small sailing boat. You think there is going to be a bad storm. You want to go back to the harbour. Your friend doesn't want to go back. Work out the conversation between the two of you.

Unit Fifteen

1 Expressing doubt.

There are many ways of doing this.
You can say only:
I doubt it or
I don't really think so.

Sometimes of course, you have to say more:
It may rain, but I doubt it.
I don't really think it's going to rain.

Read this advertisement. Do you doubt anything it says?

New miracle language pills

Do you want to learn a foreign language? Do you want to have perfect pronunciation? Try Dr Gullible's Miracle Language Pills. Take one a day for a month and you can learn a language perfectly! If you take two a day, you'll learn the language in half the time. Millions of people have already tried this new miracle language method. And it works! What's more, these pills are now used by many famous people who have to learn languages. People like Ernest Getahead, successful young businessman:

> 'I travel all over the world. I used to buy phrase books and have boring lessons. Not any more. Now I take Dr G's pills. Now I speak Chinese, Japanese, Russian, Spanish, German, French, Italian and Portuguese! All perfectly. And all thanks to Dr G's miracle language pills.'

Order now! For readers of this book there is a special offer. New jumbo English pills! Only £1,000 for 30!

2 Arguing, disagreeing, emphasising.

Notice the way June and David disagree:
I don't think we should go on.
– *Well, I do!*
I'm going to the top.
– *Well, I'm not.*

Disagree with these things in the same way:

1 I think Dr G's pills are good.
2 I'm going to buy some.
3 I've already bought some.
4 I don't think they're bad.
5 I believe the advertisement.
6 I'll tell my friends to buy some.
7 I'm sure they're good.
8 I believed what Ernest Getahead said about them.

3 Using emphasis.

In the same way you can emphasise what you say – as June and David do:
I don't think we should go on.
I really don't.
I'm sure there's going to be a storm.
I really am.

Finish these sentences:

1 I'm not afraid of getting wet. I ________ .
2 I'm sure it will rain. I ________ .
3 I don't like the look of those clouds. I ________ .
4 I took some of Dr G's pills and they worked! They ________.
5 I speak ten languages perfectly now. I ________.
6 And I've learnt them with Dr G's pills. I ________.
7 If you take them, you'll learn languages, too. You ________.
8 You won't be disappointed! You ________.

Unit Fifteen

E

1 What has gone wrong?

Sometimes a whole line or more from one of these articles has got mixed up with the other. Read both articles and say where you think this has happened.

TRAGIC LOVE STORY WINS FILM PRIZE

The Bridge is a simple but
deeply moving film about a poor
bank clerk in Paris at the end
of the last century. One day
5 he meets a beautiful woman on
a bridge over the Seine. She
tells him she is married to the
tree lying across the line. He
tells her he is an artist. They
10 fall in love. One day she asks
him to paint her portrait. He
promises to do this. But he
is afraid that the woman won't
be a very terrible accident if
15 out he isn't really an artist at
all. He jumps off the bridge where
they first met and drowns in the
river because he is so afraid of
losing her love. The woman is
20 where the tree was. A lot of
doesn't come to see her any more.
At the end of the film we find out
that she lied to him, too. She
is really a poor woman who works
25 in a dress shop.

Boy prevents train disaster

Donald Harding, 15, of Hassocks,
near Brighton, was walking home
yesterday evening after a bad
storm. He stopped for a moment
5 on a bridge over the railway
line from London to Brighton.
To his surprise he saw a big
British Ambassador in Paris. He
jumped down from the bridge and
10 ran along the line, shouting and
waving his arms. He knew that a
train was coming along the line
and he was sure that there would
love him any more when she finds
15 the train hit the tree. The
train was just coming out of a
tunnel when the driver saw him.
'We stopped just in time.
The line bends just before the place
20 broken-hearted when her lover
people could have been killed,'
the driver said later.

2 Questions.

1 Explain what the film is about and what happens in it.
2 Why do you think it is called a 'tragic love story'?
3 Why did the boy jump off the bridge?
4 Explain how he prevented a disaster.

THE VISITOR

EPISODE FIFTEEN

'You must come with me now, Mr Redford. Quickly! There isn't much time!' Tan-Lin said. But at first Tony didn't hear her. He was still staring at the machine with Liz's face. It was standing there like a frozen statue. Its eyes were still staring out lifelessly. Some smoke was coming from one of its eyes.
'How did you know what to do . . . I mean, how did you stop it?' Tony asked.
'I can explain that later, Mr Redford. Later! But first we have to get out of here. Through the window!'
At first Tony couldn't believe his ears.
'What are you talking about? We have to wait here. The police will want to ask us a lot of questions about . . . about this thing here!' He pointed to the robot. It looked and smelt more like a burnt-out machine than a human being now.
'No, Mr Redford. We can't wait for the police and all their questions. It will take far too long. Come with me!' Tan-Lin gripped his arm and pulled him out of bed. Her grip was as strong as the grip of the terrible machine with Liz's face.
'But I can't! I mean, my clothes!' he said. He was wearing only a thin cotton hospital nightgown. She pulled him with her towards the window. She could hear noises at the end of the long hospital corridor. She knew that people were coming.
'We can't wait!' she said. She carried him out of the window and down a fire escape just outside the window. When they got to the street below, a few people were walking along it. They stopped and stared at the strange sight.

One of them told a newspaper about it later.
'I was walking along the street when I suddenly saw a tall, thin woman. She was carrying a man in her arms, almost like a baby. He was wearing some kind of nightgown. At first I thought I was dreaming. But she pushed him into a car and drove away. I even heard her say "I'm glad I learnt to drive these primitive machines of yours." Those were her exact words. She had a strange accent. It wasn't very strong but I don't think she was English,' the man said.

Tan-Lin took Tony first to his flat, where he got some clothes.
'And now we must go to Southampton,' she said. Tony followed her back to the car.
'Why do you want to go there? I mean, shouldn't you tell the police about Shandor?' he asked.
'There's no time for that. I've told you that before. We must get to Shandor before he finds out what has happened to his robot. And Shandor isn't a case for your police, Mr Redford. His case is for other people, somewhere else, not here,' she answered. They got into her car and drove through the night, towards Southampton.

Question.

What do you think Tan-Lin means when she says 'Shandor isn't a case for your police'?

Unit Sixteen

A

Today in *Theme of the Week* we hear the story of Olivia Standler, a famous novelist. Once, a long time ago, she had to make a very difficult decision.

It was during the war. I mean the Second World War, of course. I was very young and I was working in London. One evening I was waiting for a bus. A young soldier was standing next to me in the queue. He started a conversation. I didn't want to talk at first. But when we got on the bus, he sat down next to me. That was how it all began. He had only ten days to go before he had to go back to the army. We spent them together. Things like that often happened during the war. 'War-time romances' they called them.

A few days before he went back, he asked me to marry him. He wanted to do it the next day. It was a difficult decision . . . very difficult . . . I think I loved him and I think he loved me, too. But I said no. I just wasn't sure. We had a terrible argument about it. I felt very bad about it afterwards. I felt it was all my fault.

I remember the last time I saw him. We went to the station together. We stood on the platform without saying a word. He got on the train and it pulled out slowly. He was waving sadly and he looked very unhappy. I'll never forget it. That was the last time I ever saw him. He went to Italy a few days afterwards. That's where he was killed. In November, 1944. He was only twenty-two.

It's a pity he died so young. And it's a pity we didn't have more time together. I'm sorry we had that terrible argument before he left. It ruined our last few days.

Perhaps I shouldn't have said no. I mean, perhaps I should have married him. I often think about it all even now, all these years later. What should I have done? I often ask myself that question. But I still can't find the answer.

Answer.

1 What was the difficult decision Olivia Standler had to make?
2 What was her decision?
3 How do you think she feels about it now?
4 Describe how she and the soldier met.
5 What happened then?
6 What was their argument about?
7 Why did she feel so bad about it?
8 Describe the last time she saw him.
9 What happened in November 1944?
10 What is the question Olivia has often asked herself since then?
11 What do you think she should have done?
12 Why?

1 Stop and look.

It's a pity we didn't have more time together.
I'm sorry we had that argument.

Which one of these sentences shows that Olivia thinks it was her fault?
Which one shows she feels sorry about it but doesn't think it was her fault?

2 Questions.

You went on a picnic last week. These things (1–7) happened. About which of them would you say *It is/was a pity . . .?* Make full sentences.

1 The weather was bad.
2 It rained very hard.
3 A bee stung one of the other people.
4 I didn't bring an umbrella.
5 I had an argument with one of my friends afterwards.
6 I shouted at him and called him an idiot.
7 Afterwards the car broke down.

3 Stop and look.

What *should* I *have done?*
Perhaps I *shouldn't have said* no.
I mean, I *should have married* him.

This is one way of talking about mistakes in the past. You can also use it to give your opinion about people's past actions:
I think she *should have married* him.
I don't think she *should have married* him.

4 What does Olivia say?

Here are some more things that happened. What do you think Olivia says about them now, all these years later?

1 Olivia didn't write to him for a long time.
2 She didn't wave when he left.
3 He wrote but she never answered his letters.
4 She finally wrote a letter but she didn't send it.
5 She carried it around with her.
6 When she finally posted it, it was too late. He was killed before it arrived.

5 What about you?

Think of mistakes or difficult decisions you have made. What should you have done? What shouldn't you have done?

Unit Sixteen

C

1 Listen to the dialogue.

It is 1944. Olivia is talking to a good friend of hers, Marcia.

OLIVIA: Donald has asked me to marry him.
MARCIA: Has he? Congratulations! That's wonderful!
OLIVIA: Is it?
MARCIA: Well . . . yes . . . don't you think it is?
OLIVIA: I'm not sure. I'm really not.
MARCIA: Why not? Don't you love him?
OLIVIA: Yes . . . I think so. But is that a good reason to get married? Now? With a war going on?
MARCIA: I don't think I understand.
OLIVIA: Well, it's . . . how shall I say it . . . oh, I find it very difficult to explain!
MARCIA: Are you afraid he may be . . . may be . . .
OLIVIA: Killed? Yes, of course. But that isn't the reason.
MARCIA: Well, what is it, then?
OLIVIA: It's just that I feel that . . . how can I put it . . . if there weren't a war on, things would be different. We'd have more time together. More time to decide. How can I be sure I really love him? Or that he loves me? I sometimes think he wants to get married now because he thinks it may be his last chance.
MARCIA: To do what?
OLIVIA: To get married, of course.
MARCIA: Oh, I see. I mean, I think I'm beginning to understand now.
OLIVIA: What would you do if you were me? I mean, would you . . . do you think I should . . .
MARCIA: It's hard to say. I just don't know.
OLIVIA: Neither do I. That's the problem!

2 Answer.

1 What does Olivia find difficult to explain?
2 Why isn't she sure if she should marry Donald?
3 Why does she think Donald wants to get married?

3 Ask and answer.

What ________ you do if you ________ Olivia?
________ you marry Donald if you ________ Olivia?

4 Look and find.

1 What would you say when someone says something like 'I passed my exams yesterday' or 'My wife has just had a baby'?
2 You are trying to explain something but can't find the right words. What do you say just before you try?
3 You have a difficult decision. You want advice from someone. What do you ask?

5 Explain these words.

1 MARCIA: *Has* he?
2 OLIVIA: *Is* it?
3 OLIVIA: Neither *do* I.

Unit Sixteen

D

1 What would you do if you were in these situations?

It is 9.10. You work in an office with a girl called Kate. The boss doesn't like her. She's late. The boss asks you, 'Where's Kate?' Would you say, 'She isn't here. She'll be back soon'? Or would you say, 'She's late'? Remember, if the boss finds out she's late, she may lose her job. If he finds out you're lying, you may lose your job!

You are in a dark street. You see a man in front of you. He has a gun and is robbing two people. He can't see you. What would you do? Would you try to stop him? Or would you run away?

You're in a crowded bus. You have a seat. An old lady gets on. She can't find a seat. You're very tired. Nobody else gets up and gives her a seat. What would you do? Would you give her your seat? Or would you just sit there? Or would you perhaps do something else? What?

2 Stop and look.

If the boss *asked* me about Kate, I *would* ________.

If I *saw* the man and he *couldn't see* me, I *would* ________.

If I *were* in the bus and an old lady *got* on, I *would* ________.

This form is called the *conditional*. We use it to talk about unreal situations. These situations are unreal because you aren't really in them. Look at the form of verb after *if*. What do you notice about it?

3 Use the verbs in brackets to make sentences or questions.

Example: (*do, see*) What ________ you ________ if you ________ a man with a gun?
= What *would you do* if you *saw* a man with a gun?

1 (*do, have*) What ________ you ________ if you ________ a million pounds?
2 (*have, go*) If I ________ that much money, I ________ ________ on a long holiday.
3 (*give, get on*) ________ you ________ your seat to that old lady if she ________ ________the bus?
4 (*run away, see*) I think I ________ ________ ________ if I ________ a man with a gun.
5 (*can, phone*) Of course, if I ________ find a telephone, I ________ ________ the police.
6 (*ask, say*) If the boss ________ me about Kate, I ________ ________ nothing.

Unit Sixteen

E

1 Listen to the dialogue, then answer these questions:

1 Olivia apologises for something. For what? How? When?
2 What do you think she wants to say but can't?
3 Why can't she say it?

It is 22nd May, 1944. Donald and Olivia are at the station.

DONALD: Well . . . it's time to . . .
OLIVIA: I . . . I want . . . I mean . . . I hope . . .
DONALD: Yes?
OLIVIA: I hope you're not angry. About the argument, I mean.
DONALD: No. Don't worry about it. It was my fault. I shouldn't have . . .
OLIVIA: It was both our faults.
DONALD: I think I should get on now.
OLIVIA: Goodbye, Donald.
DONALD: Goodbye Olivia. You . . . I hope . . .
OLIVIA: Yes?
DONALD: Please write.
OLIVIA: I will. I promise. You write, too.
DONALD: Yes, I will.
OLIVIA: Take care of yourself.
DONALD: I will.
OLIVIA: Have you got everything?
(Someone blows a whistle; the train is ready to leave. Donald gets on the train.)
OLIVIA: Well, good luck and . . . Donald . . . perhaps when you come back we can . . .
(The train begins to leave.)
DONALD: What? Sorry? I can't hear you.
OLIVIA: (*Shouting.*) Perhaps when you come back we can get marr . . .
DONALD: What? I can't hear!
(The train leaves.)

2 Answer as Donald does.

OLIVIA: Please write.
DONALD: Yes, I *will*.
OLIVIA: Have you got everything?
DONALD: Yes, I *have*.

1 Take care of yourself.
2 I hope you've enjoyed your holiday.
3 I hope you still love me.
4 Please phone.
5 Don't get into trouble.
6 Have you got my address and phone number?

WHAT PEOPLE SAY

Now turn to page 106 and listen to the tape. Find out what people say about winning a million pounds and what they would take to a desert island.

THE VISITOR

EPISODE SIXTEEN

It was almost dawn. Tony and Tan-Lin were standing on a hill overlooking the sea. They were near Southampton.
'Why have we come here?' Tony asked.
'Shandor's factory is on the other side of this hill. Every morning at dawn, a helicopter flies from the factory to Shandor's yacht. I don't know exactly where it is. But we're going to find out soon.' Tony didn't really understand but he had another question.
'Where are you from? If you're a visitor, where did you come from in the first place?'

Tan-Lin smiled and pointed up to the dark sky. She pointed up to a group of stars in the east. It took Tony a few moments to understand.
'Are you trying to tell me you come from another planet?'
'Yes, Mr Redford. And so does Shandor. From the same planet, far far away. And on our planet, we use highly developed robots for certain kinds of jobs. These robots look almost like us. Shandor was trained to make those robots. And five years ago he was sent here to find out more about how robots are used here, on your planet.' Tony stared at her with a surprised look on his face.
'Yes, that is right, Mr Redford. We sometimes send people here to find out what you are doing. You are far behind us in many ways. But not in all. For example, you now have terrible weapons which not even we have. Or rather, it is forbidden for us to make them.'
'And why have you come here, Tan-Lin?'
'Shandor has broken our laws. It is forbidden for us to kill. It is forbidden for us to interfere in the affairs of another planet. Shandor is very dangerous. He has stolen Government secrets. These are secret plans. Plans to make more terrible weapons. Perhaps Shandor is planning to make those weapons himself. Or perhaps he wants to sell the information to other governments. We do not know. But he has broken our law and I must find him and take him back. I have known for a long time that he is here. But not exactly where. Now I can find out. Listen!'

Tony heard the sound of a helicopter. Then he saw it. It rose into the sky in front of them and flew out over the sea to the west. Then Tony heard another sound. It was different. It was a low, humming noise. He looked behind him and saw a round ball of light moving towards them. It was flying very low. The ball of light landed in front of them. Tony saw it was some kind of spaceship, a flying saucer.

A small door opened in the metal skin of the spaceship. Tan-Lin walked towards it. Then Tony saw another figure. It was standing in the door, waiting. The figure looked something like a man. But it had a square head and only one large eye. Tan-Lin spoke to it in a strange language. Tony saw it was a robot. It turned and went back into the spaceship. Tan-Lin looked back at Tony.
'If you come with me, Mr Redford, you will see things which nobody will believe.'
Tony followed her through the door and into the spaceship. It rose into the sky and followed the helicopter out to sea. The sun was slowly rising behind them, a bright red ball in the still dark sky.

Questions.

1 Explain why Tan-Lin has come to this planet.
2 What do you think is going to happen now?

The Party

A

Claire Walton is working at home on a Sunday afternoon. The phone rings. It is an old friend.

CLAIRE: Hello.
MICK: Hello, Claire. This is Mick.
CLAIRE: Mick! Nice to hear from you again. How are you?
MICK: Fine, thanks. And you?
CLAIRE: Oh, not so bad. I've been very busy but I'm going away on holiday soon.
MICK: Good. Listen. I'm phoning because I want to invite you to a party. At our new house. And . . .
CLAIRE: New house? Really?
MICK: Yes. We've moved. That's why we're giving the party. Can you come?
CLAIRE: Well, that depends. When is it?
MICK: This Saturday evening.
CLAIRE: Well . . . I'm going away on Sunday morning. Very early. Will the party go on very late?
MICK: Until two in the morning. But you don't have to stay that long. Well? What about it?
CLAIRE: All right. I'll come. But I'd like to bring a present. Something for your new house. What would you like?
MICK: Nothing. I mean, don't bring anything. It isn't necessary.
CLAIRE: But I'd still like . . .
MICK: Just bring yourself! I'm looking forward to seeing you again. It's been a long time!
CLAIRE: Yes, it has. I'm looking forward to seeing you, too. And your new house. Uh . . . when does the party start?
MICK: Come any time after eight. All right?
CLAIRE: Yes. Oh, by the w . . .
MICK: Bye! See you on Saturday evening.
CLAIRE: Wait a moment, Mick. You haven't . . . Mick? Are you still there? You haven't given me your new address' Hello? Mick? Hello?

Answer.

1 Why is Mick phoning?
2 Why is he giving a party?
3 When is he giving it?
4 Why doesn't Claire want to stay until it ends?
5 Mick forgets something important. What?

Ask and answer.

1 ________ Claire been very busy?
2 When ________ she going away on holiday?
3 When ________ the party end?
4 ________ Claire have to stay until the end?
5 ________ it necessary to bring a present?
6 ________ Claire know Mick's new address?

What do you think?

Which does 'I'm looking forward to seeing you' mean?

a I'm sure I will see you.
b I'm happy when I think about seeing you.
c I know I will see you but not for a long time.

1 Stop and look.

Mick is looking forward to *seeing* Claire again. She is looking forward to *going* on holiday.

What do you notice about the form of the verb after *look forward to?*

Make more sentences with the words in brackets:

1 Claire is looking forward to (*go*) away.
2 She is looking forward to (*see*) some of her old friends.
3 She is looking forward to (*talk*) to them.
4 What are you looking forward to (*do*) on your holiday?

Now talk about some of the things you are looking forward to doing in the next few weeks or months.

2 Notice the difference between *because* and *That's why*.

Mick is phoning *because* he wants to invite Claire to a party. Mick wants to invite Claire to a party. *That's why* he is phoning.

Use *because* or *That's why* in these examples.

Remember:

I can't come. I'm busy=I can't come because I'm busy.

I'm busy. I can't come =I'm busy. That's why I can't come.

1 Claire has to phone Mick. He didn't give her his new address.
2 She can't stay late. She has to get up early.
3 I can't come to the party. I won't be here.
4 I won't be here. I can't come to the party.
5 I had an accident. I'm late for work.
6 I'm late for work. I had an accident.

3 Listening practice.

Claire had Mick's phone number because he didn't change it when he moved. She phoned him. Listen to their conversation on tape. Then answer the questions.

1 Where exactly does Mick live?
2 How will Claire get there?
3 Why can't she use her car?

The Party

C

1 Who is saying what at the party? Find the conversation.

2 Think about it!

1 In one of these conversations, someone is apologising for something. For what? How does the person apologise?
2 In another conversation, someone is offering someone something. What? How?
3 In another conversation, someone is agreeing with someone. What are they saying?
4 And someone is also introducing someone to someone else. What are they saying?

1 Here are two of the conversations that are going on at the party. Look at them. Which words do you think are missing?

Conversation 1.

CLAIRE: What do you ___(1)___ , Tony?
TONY: I'm a teacher.
CLAIRE: Which ___(2)___ do you teach?
TONY: English as a Foreign Language and Business Studies. I use your programmes a ___(3)___ .
CLAIRE: ___(4)___ you? How?
TONY: Well, the class and I ___(5)___ the programme ___(6)___ and then we discuss it.
CLAIRE: And do your students ___(7)___ the programmes very interesting?
TONY: Yes, I think ___(8)___ . I mean, I think they like them very ___(9)___ .

Here are the missing words. Where do they belong?
a) watch b) first c) find d) do e) so f) lot
g) subjects h) much i) Do

Conversation 2.

MAN: How exactly did it ___(1)___ ?
WOMAN: Well, as I ___(2)___ you, I was on a skiing holiday. But I'm not very ___(3)___ at skiing. Anyway, one day I fell and ___(4)___ my leg. At first I ___(5)___ even know it was broken. But when I ___(6)___ to get up, I felt a terrible ___(7)___ in my leg.
MAN: And what ___(8)___ then?
WOMAN: Nothing. I just lay in the snow ___(9)___ two other skiers saw me.
MAN: What did they ___(10)___ ?
WOMAN: They waited with me. And then a helicopter came and ___(11)___ me to hospital.

And where do these words belong?
a) good b) pain c) until d) happen
e) happened f) told g) took h) broke
i) didn't j) tried k) do

2 Listen to the two conversations.

THE VISITOR

EPISODE SEVENTEEN

The spaceship was round and flat, like a saucer. It looked small from the outside. But Tony was surprised at how big it seemed from the inside. The robot turned. Its one big round eye was shining brightly.

'You are welcome here, Mr Redford,' it said in a mechanical voice but perfect English. Tan-Lin operated the controls. The robot sat behind her. Through a round window Tony could see the sea below. They were flying just above the waves, and they were rising and falling with them.

'The helicopter is a kilometre ahead of us. It has just landed on the yacht,' Tan-Lin told Tony. She pointed to a radar screen.

In his cabin on the yacht, Shandor was listening to Harlan. There was a worried look on the older man's face. And Shandor looked angry.

'What has gone wrong now, you fool?'

'I'm not sure, Mr Shandor. The operator was programmed exactly as you instructed. It should have gone to the hospital and killed Redford yesterday evening. But it hasn't come back. We've heard nothing from it!'

Shandor stood up. For a moment Harlan thought he was going to hit him. But he didn't. His cold blue eyes flashed with anger.

'I told you there must be no more mistakes!'

Suddenly he stopped.

'What's that noise?' he asked.

Harlan listened. At first he didn't hear anything. But then he did. It was a low, whistling noise, almost like the wind. But it rose and became louder.

Shandor and Harlan ran up to the deck. The strange noise was getting louder and louder. Other men ran out on to the deck and looked up into the sky. The spaceship came in low, just over the waves, from the direction of the rising sun. The whistling noise was very loud now. Shandor and the other men put their fingers in their ears to stop the noise. But it didn't help. One by one they fell over on the deck and lay there stiffly, without moving. The spaceship was just above them, turning slowly in the air. The whistling noise stopped and the spaceship landed on the deck.

'Are they dead?' Tony asked. They were standing on the deck and looking at the men on it.

'No, of course not. They have been . . . what do you say . . . "stunned"'.

'Stunned? By what?'

'By the noise we made. They will wake up soon with terrible headaches. They will never know what has happened. But Shandor will not be here. And his robots and factories will be destroyed. There will be a strange fire in exactly five minutes. This yacht will be destroyed, too. But nobody will die,' Tan-Lin said.

The robot put Shandor in the spaceship. Then Tan-Lin and the robot put Harlan and the other men in a boat. The spaceship rose from the deck of the yacht a few minutes later. Tony looked down at it from a window. Suddenly it caught fire and exploded. Shandor was in a chair next to the robot. He was held there by a beam of light, like an invisible chain. He opened his eyes. There was hatred in them. But he didn't speak.

It was still early morning when they landed again. They were on a beach near Southampton. There were no people or houses around them. Tony got out and stood on the sand. Tan-Lin came to the door of the spaceship.

'We must leave now, Mr Redford. We have a long journey. A very long one.' She held out her hand. Tony shook it. He didn't know what to say. Tan-Lin went back into the spaceship. It flew out low over the waves at first. Then it suddenly went up high in the direction of the rising sun. Tony watched it.

'Nobody's going to believe this! Nobody!' he thought.

WHAT PEOPLE SAY

What people say about their jobs

(Use this material when you are studying Unit 4 – see page 23.)

1 Look at these pictures:

Now listen to the tape. Three of the people in the pictures say what they like about their jobs. Write in the corner of the picture who speaks first (1), who speaks second (2) and who speaks third (3).

2 Next listen and tick (√) the correct sentence.

Mike likes
- a working in a factory.
- b doing the same thing all the time.
- c doing something different all the time.

Vera likes
- a being shut away from people.
- b talking to people.
- c working by herself.

Barbara likes
- a telling stories.
- b interviewing people.
- c making the news.

3 Next all four of the people in the pictures say what they don't like about their jobs. Listen to the tape and say if these sentences are true or false.

a Mike says he doesn't like working long hours. True/False

b Vera says she doesn't like people who are rude. True/False

c Barbara says she doesn't like getting up for work. True/False

d John says his job is boring. True/False

4 Listen to what Mike does in his spare time. Tick what he does.

Mike
- a repairs cars.
- b goes to discos.
- c watches TV.

Now listen to Vera, Barbara and John saying what they do in their spare time. Tick what they do.

Vera
- a listens to the radio.
- b makes cakes.
- c knits.

Barbara
- a watches TV.
- b cooks.
- c plays golf.

John
- a goes to pubs.
- b teaches.
- c enjoys music.

WHAT PEOPLE SAY

What people say about their holidays

(Use this material when you are studying Unit 8 – see page 47.)

1 Look at these pictures:

Elise is a writer.

Barbara.

Rory is a teacher.

Irene works in a fish and chip shop.

Mike.

You are going to hear these people talking about their holidays. Listen and write down where each person went.

a Elise went to ____________________ .

b Rory went to ____________________ .

c Barbara went to ____________________ .

d Mike went to the ____________________ .

e Irene went to the ____________________ .

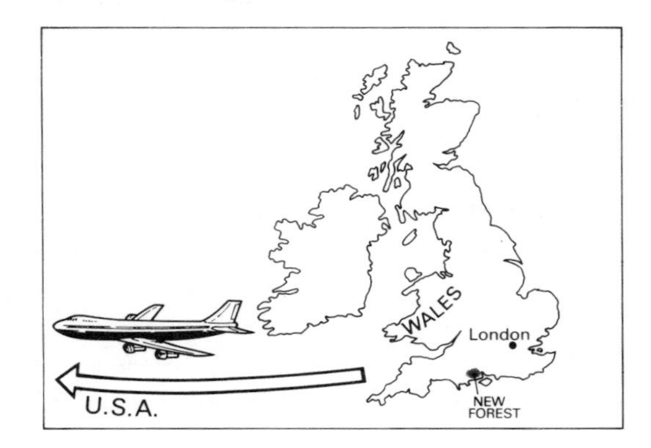

2 Now listen to what each person did on holiday. Say if these sentences are true or false.

a i Elise went to the theatre.
True / False
ii She worked hard.
True / False

b i Rory stayed in a hotel.
True / False
ii The weather was good.
True / False

c i Barbara went away for two weeks.
True / False
ii She stayed with friends.
True / False

d i Mike went camping.
True / False
ii He went sight-seeing.
True / False

e i Irene likes to relax on holiday.
True / False
ii She wants to go abroad.
True / False

WHAT PEOPLE SAY

What people say about keeping fit

(Use this material when you are studying Unit 12 – see page 71.)

1 Listen to what these people say about keeping fit and complete the sentences.

a Irene If they don't __________ so hard they shouldn't eat so much.

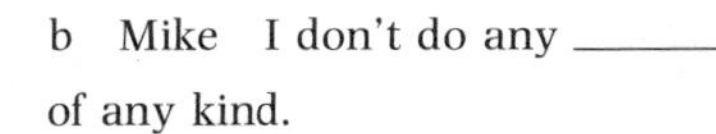

b Mike I don't do any __________ of any kind.

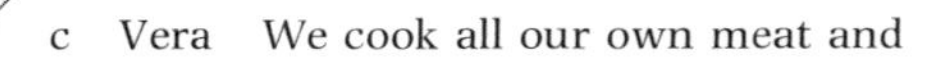

c Vera We cook all our own meat and __________ .

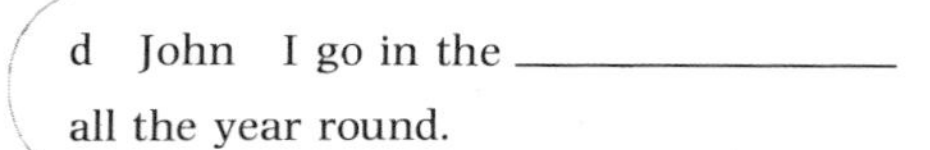

d John I go in the __________ all the year round.

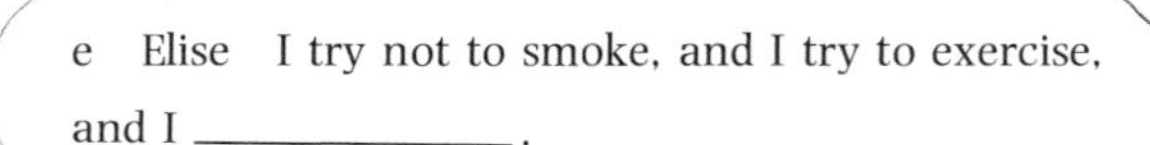

e Elise I try not to smoke, and I try to exercise, and I __________ .

2 Now listen and say if these sentences are true or false.

a i Irene does nothing in particular to keep fit.
True / False
ii She says people should diet.
True / False

b i Mike does exercises to keep fit.
True / False

c i Vera doesn't take vitamin tablets.
True / False
ii She eats a lot of frozen food.
True / False

d i John goes swimming.
True / False
ii He swims once a month.
True / False

e i Elise tries not to eat sweets or drink a lot of wine.
True / False
ii She sleeps for ten hours every night.
True / False
iii She goes swimming.
True / False

WHAT PEOPLE SAY

What people say about winning a million pounds

(Use the material on this page when you are studying Unit 16 – see page 95.)

1 If Mike, Elise, Barbara and John won a million pounds each, what would they do with it?
Listen and tick the correct sentences.

a Mike would
- i buy motor bikes.
- ii invest the money in a Building Society.
- iii have a party.

b Elise would
- i phone her friends to tell them.
- ii get advice about what to do with the money.
- iii buy a Rolls Royce.

c Barbara would
- i buy a new car.
- ii throw the money away.
- iii give the money away.

d John would
- i buy a large house.
- ii live in a town.
- iii buy some good furniture.

What would they take to a desert island?

2 Mike, Elise and Barbara say what three things they would take to a desert island. Listen to them and write their names under the picture of what they would take.

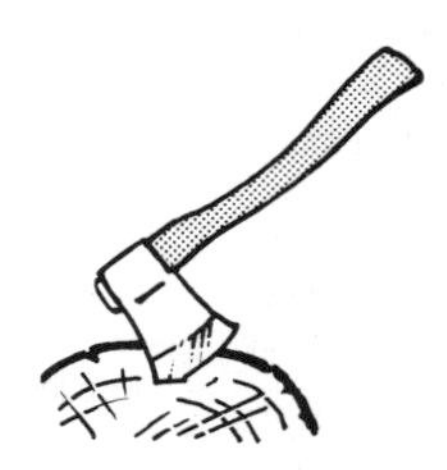

Review

UNIT ONE

<table>
<tr><td>What did</td><td>her husband
the people
the object</td><td>look like?</td></tr>
</table>

<table>
<tr><td>She</td><td>met him</td><td>two weeks</td><td rowspan="3">ago.</td></tr>
<tr><td>It</td><td>ended</td><td>six years</td></tr>
<tr><td>I
He
She
We
They</td><td>got up
had breakfast</td><td>3 hours
half an hour</td></tr>
</table>

<table>
<tr><td>He
She</td><td>was</td><td rowspan="2">tall.
short.
handsome.</td><td rowspan="2"></td></tr>
<tr><td>They</td><td>were</td></tr>
<tr><td>He
She
They</td><td>had</td><td>curly
straight
dark
short
long</td><td>hair.</td></tr>
<tr><td>It</td><td>was</td><td>long.
thin.
round.
flat.</td><td></td></tr>
</table>

<table>
<tr><td rowspan="3">How long ago</td><td rowspan="3">did</td><td>you
he
she
they</td><td>get up?
have breakfast?</td></tr>
<tr><td>Judy</td><td>meet her husband?</td></tr>
<tr><td>the war</td><td>end?</td></tr>
</table>

UNIT TWO

<table>
<tr><td>Are</td><td>you
they</td><td rowspan="2">interested in</td><td rowspan="2">music?
sport?
tennis?</td></tr>
<tr><td>Is</td><td>he
she</td></tr>
</table>

<table>
<tr><td>I'm (I am)
He's
She's
We're
You're
They're</td><td>not</td><td rowspan="2">interested in</td><td rowspan="2">music.
sport.
tennis.</td></tr>
<tr><td>He
She</td><td>isn't</td></tr>
</table>

<table>
<tr><td>Do</td><td>you
they</td><td rowspan="2">enjoy
hate</td><td rowspan="2">listening to music?
going on holiday?
watching sport?
Technical College?
folk music?</td></tr>
<tr><td>Does</td><td>Clive
she</td></tr>
</table>

<table>
<tr><td>I
He
She
They</td><td>would</td><td>like to
prefer to</td><td rowspan="4">go to the theatre.
play tennis
stay in bed.
watch television.</td></tr>
<tr><td>I
They</td><td>(don't)</td><td>want to
hope to
have to</td></tr>
<tr><td rowspan="2">He
She</td><td colspan="2">wants to
hopes to
has to</td></tr>
<tr><td>doesn't</td><td>want to
hope to
have to</td></tr>
</table>

<table>
<tr><td rowspan="2">I
We
They
He
She</td><td>don't</td><td rowspan="2">enjoy</td><td rowspan="3">listening to music.
going on holiday.
watching sport.
Technical College.
folk music.</td></tr>
<tr><td>doesn't</td></tr>
<tr><td>He
She</td><td colspan="2">enjoys</td></tr>
</table>

Do	you they	like to	lie stay	in the sun? in bed all day?
Does	he she	like	lying staying	

Would	you he she they	like to prefer to	go to the theatre? play tennis? stay in bed all day? watch television?
Do	you they	want to hope to have to	
Does	he she		

UNIT THREE

Would Could Can	you he she they	wait a moment? show me some watches? tell me the time?	Of course. Certainly.

What	is	she he	going to	do? buy?
	are	you we they		

Open	that safe.
Put up	your hands.
Stop	that.

I You We They	(don't)	need	a	new car. bigger house. lot of things.
He She	(doesn't)			
He She		needs		

You must	open stop	it.

Who	is		younger? taller? stronger?
		more	intelligent? attractive?

Donald He The chimpanzee	is		younger taller	than	Ponzo. Donald. him. the chimpanzee.
		more	intelligent attractive		

<table>
<tr><td>Which watch</td><td>is</td><td>bigger?
smaller?
cheaper?
more expensive?
better?</td></tr>
</table>

<table>
<tr><td>This</td><td>watch
one</td><td>is</td><td>bigger
smaller
cheaper
more expensive
better</td><td>than that one.</td></tr>
</table>

<table>
<tr><td>I'm (I am)
You're
We're
They're
He's
She's</td><td>not</td><td rowspan="3">going to</td><td rowspan="3">give up work.
buy a new car.
buy a bigger house.</td></tr>
<tr><td>He
She</td><td>isn't</td></tr>
<tr><td>You
We
They</td><td>aren't</td></tr>
</table>

UNIT FOUR

<table>
<tr><td>What</td><td>should</td><td>I
you</td><td>wear?
buy?</td></tr>
</table>

<table>
<tr><td>I
You
He
She
We
They</td><td>should

shouldn't</td><td>wear a tie.
buy a white shirt.
change her clothes.</td></tr>
</table>

<table>
<tr><td>Do</td><td>you
they
we</td><td rowspan="2">think</td><td rowspan="2">I
you
he
she
we
they</td><td rowspan="2">should</td><td rowspan="2">wear jeans to work?
buy some new clothes?
get a job?</td></tr>
<tr><td>Does</td><td>he
she</td></tr>
</table>

<table>
<tr><td>I
We
They</td><td>(don't)</td><td rowspan="2">think</td><td rowspan="2">you
they
we
he
she</td><td rowspan="2">should.</td></tr>
<tr><td>He
She</td><td>(doesn't)</td></tr>
</table>

Why	shouldn't	he she we they women	drink coffee? be interested in cooking? smoke cigarettes? wear jeans?

How long	have	you they	been	a doctor? in Brighton? with the same company?
	has	he she	had	that car? a bike? the same job?

I've (I have) We've You've They've	been	a doctor in Brighton with the same company	for	30 years. 6 months. a long time.
He's (He has) She's	had	this car a bike the same job		

UNIT FIVE

Can	I	have my money back? pay by cheque?
	you	deliver it please?

Yes, of course.
It depends where you live.

I'd (I would)	like	a radio/cassette player. the cheaper one. the best one.

Mount Everest He 1976 Sue	is	the	highest mountain happiest child best summer most interesting person	in	the	world. three. century. room.
	was			of	this	

Who is the		tallest? heaviest? youngest? oldest?
	most	beautiful? handsome?

Which is the	best? worst? biggest? smallest? cheapest? most expensive?

UNIT SIX

Stockport Killbrae	is in	the north of England. Scotland.

London Brighton Killbrae	is a	city. town. village.

<table>
<tr><td rowspan="2">Brighton</td><td rowspan="2">is</td><td>smaller</td><td rowspan="2">than</td><td>London.</td></tr>
<tr><td>bigger</td><td>Killbrae.</td></tr>
</table>

Stockport Brighton	is isn't	as	big interesting	as	Brighton. London.

<table>
<tr><td rowspan="2">How</td><td>much</td><td>money
industry
work</td><td>is</td><td rowspan="2">there in Killbrae?</td></tr>
<tr><td>many</td><td>factories
jobs
towns</td><td>are</td></tr>
</table>

Very	little. few.

How long	have you been	living in Killbrae? working for that company?

I have (I've) He has (He's) She has (She's)	been living been working	in Killbrae	for 6 years/months. since 1979.

UNIT SEVEN

There It	will be	a few showers. bright. sunny. warmer. colder. windy. cloudy.

It won't (will not)	last much longer. rain tomorrow.

<table>
<tr><td rowspan="4">I'll (I will)</td><td>pay you back</td><td rowspan="2">tomorrow.</td></tr>
<tr><td>get some</td></tr>
<tr><td>always</td><td>love you.</td></tr>
<tr><td>never</td><td>leave you.</td></tr>
</table>

When	will	it end? the cold weather stop? you be back?

<table>
<tr><td>The weather</td><td rowspan="2">has been cold</td><td>since</td><td>last Monday.</td></tr>
<tr><td>It</td><td>for</td><td>5 days.</td></tr>
</table>

The cold weather	started	five days ago.

It will (It'll)	be	warmer	tomorrow. later.
You will (You'll)	see	the sun	
There will (There'll)	be	more about this	

The	minimum	temperature	will be	3 degrees	below	zero.
	maximum				above	freezing.

UNIT EIGHT

I	usually sometimes	go	by	bus. car. train. bike. plane.
			on	foot. my bike.
			in	my car.

How long does it (usually) take you to	get to work? go to school? have breakfast?

It (usually) takes me	10 minutes. an hour. a few minutes.

If I take the 7.26 when will I arrive in London?

If you	take do leave	the 7.26 the exercise now	you'll (you will)	arrive in London at 8.32. understand. catch your train.

UNIT NINE

She	is going plans intends	to	visit Australia. star in a film. take a holiday.

What	do are	you	intend going plan	to do?

It's Tell us about	the	plane film pilot boy	which who	turned back. you're going to make. landed safely. enjoyed the storm.
Talk to This is				

The plane Thousands They I	had to	turn back. stand. use binoculars. pay high prices for tickets. wait outside the stadium. get some fresh air. stop.

The crowd They A lot of people You I	couldn't could not	get into the stadium. find seats. see the race. get a ticket for under £40. believe there were so many people.

UNIT TEN

May	I we	have your order now, please? sit here? open the window? use the phone? come in? leave before the end?

I wonder	if	it will come soon? the waiter has seen us? those seats are free? they've overcharged us?
	where	the waiter is? the menu is? the food is?
	how much	the bill will be?

How would you like it?

I'd (I would) like mine	rare. medium. well-done.

I'll have (I will have)	the lamb chops. the steak. the same.

The food It	tastes looks smells	good. bad. strange. terrible. wonderful. delicious.
The vegetables They	taste look smell	

First	cut fry	the	beef into small pieces. carrots and onions.
Then	heat cook		the cider on a low flame. for three hours.
After that	add		the stock cube. the mushrooms.
Next	put		everything into a big pot.

UNIT ELEVEN

Why don't we	tell the police? phone a garage?

I He It	may	be	late. wrong. a detective. a bomb. dangerous.
It He			explode. come tomorrow. have a gun. kill you.

Let's (Let us)	tell the police. have a look. leave the car. stop it and ask for a lift.

Who	stole the diamonds?
	carried out the operation?
	exploded the bomb?
	arrested the man and woman?
	interviewed them?

Do you think	he's a detective? it will explode? it's dangerous? we should kill her? it came from the sea? we should phone a garage?

I think we should	tell the police try to repair the engine.

The	money	was found	on the floor.
	cat	was killed	yesterday.
	diamonds	were stolen	a few months ago.
	room	was decorated	last year.
	letters	were sent	here by mistake.

The	diamonds	were stolen by	a man and a woman.
	operation	was carried out by	a team of surgeons.
	bomb	was exploded by	Army experts.
	man and woman	were arrested by	the police.
		were interviewed by	a detective.

UNIT TWELVE

I	never used used	to	play tennis. smoke a lot. stay at home all day. take the car. cycle to work.

He's started	drinking. smoking. eating fresh vegetables. doing yoga exercises.

How long have you had it?	
Have you had this trouble before?	Yes, I had it last year.
Have you seen a doctor about it?	Yes, I saw one a few days ago.
Mrs Taylor has sold her car.	She sold it six months ago.
She has bought a bike.	She bought it six months ago.
She has started doing yoga.	She started it a few months ago.

UNIT THIRTEEN

The group marched	slowly.
He drove	dangerously.
The police came	quickly.
You don't write very	clearly.
The police watched	quietly.
She dances	well.
You can speak	freely.
It rained	heavily.
He spoke	badly.

<table>
<tr><td>This train</td><td rowspan="2">is</td><td>very slow.</td></tr>
<tr><td>Atomic power</td><td>dangerous.</td></tr>
<tr><td>Your writing</td><td>isn't (is not)</td><td>clear.</td></tr>
<tr><td>The rain</td><td>is</td><td>heavy.</td></tr>
<tr><td>I'm (I am)</td><td>not</td><td>very good.</td></tr>
</table>

<table>
<tr><td>Will the pain go away</td><td rowspan="2">if</td><td>I take this medicine?</td></tr>
<tr><td>I'm sure you'll enjoy it</td><td>you come.</td></tr>
</table>

<table>
<tr><td>What are we going to do</td><td rowspan="3">when</td><td>there is no more oil?</td></tr>
<tr><td>Will you be at the airport</td><td>I arrive?</td></tr>
<tr><td>You can go out</td><td>the rain stops.</td></tr>
</table>

<table>
<tr><td rowspan="5">If</td><td>one explodes near a large city</td><td>many people</td><td rowspan="5">will</td><td>die.</td></tr>
<tr><td>it runs out</td><td>there</td><td>be alternative sources.</td></tr>
<tr><td>we build the station here</td><td>it</td><td>bring a lot of jobs.</td></tr>
<tr><td rowspan="2">you make that mistake again</td><td rowspan="2">I</td><td>ruin the village.</td></tr>
<tr><td>sack you.</td></tr>
</table>

UNIT FOURTEEN

Would you like me to Shall I	carry it for you? phone for a taxi? lend you the money? make you a cup of tea? pay the bill? write a letter?

I hope	the weather is good tomorrow. the train is on time. the train isn't late. it doesn't rain. I'll pass my exams. I'll find a comfortable bench. it won't happen.

She is	afraid of	being bitten by a dog. having an accident.
They are People are		failing their exams. losing their jobs.

I'm (I am) afraid	he will have an accident. I will lose my job. it will bite me. the next war will be worse.

UNIT FIFTEEN

I	doubt don't really think	it'll rain. it's dangerous. it's going to thunder.

I don't think we should go on, I'm going to the top, I think Dr G's pills are good, I'll tell my friends to buy some,	I really don't. I really am. I really do. I really will.	Well, I do. Well, I'm not. Well, I don't. Well, I won't.

I took some of Dr G's pills and they worked.	They really did.
I speak 10 languages perfectly now.	I really do.
I've learnt them with Dr G's pills.	I really have.
If you take them you'll learn languages too.	You really will.
You won't be disappointed.	You really won't.

Were you	reading a paper playing football working watching television having dinner	at 6.15? yesterday evening?

At 6 o'clock When I got up When I looked out of the window	the sun was shining. the train was carrying more than 1,000 passengers. thousands of people were watching a pop concert.

UNIT SIXTEEN

I'm sorry	I didn't smile. I waited too long. we had that argument.

I should have	married him. told him I loved him. waved. smiled. listened to him. said no. called him an idiot. shouted at him. got angry with him.
I shouldn't have	

It was a pity It's (It is) a pity	he died so young. we didn't have more time together. he never read it.

What would you do if	you were me? you won a million pounds?

If	I were you I had that much money	I would marry him. I would go on a long holiday.

If	the boss asked me about Kate	I would	lie.
	I were in the bus and an old lady got on		give her my seat.
	I saw the man and he couldn't see me		try to stop him.
	I could find a telephone	I'd	phone the police.
	I saw a man with a gun		

THE PARTY

He is She is	looking forward to	meeting Mick. seeing Claire again. going on holiday. talking to her friends.

Irregular verbs

Here is a list of irregular verbs with their past tense forms.

VERB	PAST TENSE	PARTICIPLE	UNIT
babysit	babysat	babysat	2
beat	beat	beaten	14
become	became	become	13
begin	began	began	1
bend	bent	bent	15
bite	bit	bitten	14
blow	blew	blown	15
break	broke	broken	8
build	built	built	11
catch	caught	caught	8
cost	cost	cost	3
cut	cut	cut	10
dig	dug	dug	13
fall	fell	fallen	1
feel	felt	felt	9
forget	forgot	forgotten	7
hit	hit	hit	4
hurt	hurt	hurt	12
keep	kept	kept	8
lead	led	led	11
lend	lent	lent	14
lie (in)	lay	lain	2
light	lit, lighted	lit, lighted	13
lose	lost	lost	2
make	made	made	1
rewrite	rewrote	rewritten	9
ride	rode	ridden	15
rise	rose	risen	7
sell	sold	sold	5
send	sent	sent	13
shake	shook	shaken	14
spend	spent	spent	2
spill	spilt, spilled	spilt, spilled	TP
sting	stung	stung	16
strike	struck	struck	9
throw	threw	thrown	13
upset	upset	upset	14
win	won	won	2

Wordlist

All words included in the wordlist are words which are introduced for the first time in Kernel Two. (Words which occurred in Kernel One are not listed, but may be found in the Teacher's Book.) Each entry is followed by its phonetic transcription (see *Pronunciation key*) and then the unit is given in which the word first occurs. Please note that TP stands for 'The Party'.

Pronunciation key

The following key demonstrates how the phonetics should be read so that they are pronounced correctly. This key is derived from the *Longman Dictionary of Contemporary English*.

Consonants

SYMBOL	KEY WORD
b	bag
d	day
ð	they
dʒ	job
f	find
g	give
h	hat
j	yes
k	key
l	look
m	man
n	not
ŋ	sing
p	pay
r	red
s	soon
ʃ	shop
t	tell
tʃ	chair
θ	thing
v	very
w	week
z	zoo
ʒ	television

Vowels

SYMBOL	KEY WORD
æ	hat
ɑ:	park
aɪ	time
aʊ	now
e	bed
eɪ	day
eə	chair
ə	about
əʊ	home
ɜ:	girl
i:	see
ɪ	sit
ɪə	here
ɔ:	saw
ɒ	got
ɔɪ	boy
u:	zoo
ʊ	put
ʊə	sure
ʌ	cup

Wordlist

A

- **able** / ˈeɪbəl /: **be able** 14
- **abroad** / əˈbrɔ:d / 8
- **accident** / ˈæksɪdənt / 4
- **accommodation** / əˈkɒməˈdeɪʃən / 8
- **account** / əˈkaʊnt /: **expense account** 12
- **acid** / ˈæsɪd / 13
- **act** / ækt / *v* 13
- **action** / ˈækʃən / 15
- **active** / ˈæktɪv / 5
- **activity** / ækˈtɪvɪti / 2
- **add** / æd / *v* 10
- **adjective** / ˈædʒɪktɪv / 5
- **adverb** / ˈædvɜ:b / 13
- **advice** / ədˈvaɪs / 12
- **advise** / ədˈvaɪz / *v* 12
- **aeroplane** / ˈeərəpleɪn / 2
- **affair** / əˈfeə^{r} / 15
- **afraid** (frightened) / əˈfreɪd / 9
  - **I'm afraid** (*apology*) 8
- **after** / ˈɑfte^{r} /: **run after** 14
- **afterwards** / ˈɑ:ftəwədz / 16
- **against** / əˈgenst / 13
- **age** / eɪdʒ / 5
- **ago** / əˈgəʊ / 1
- **agree** / əˈgri: / 13
- **air** / eə^{r} / *n* 2
- **airliner** / ˈeəˌlaɪnə^{r} / 9
- **alarm** / əˈlɑ:m / *n* 5
- **alone** / əˈləʊn / 15
- **along** / əˈlɒŋ / 8
- **already** / ɔ:lˈredi / 13
- **also** / ˈɔ:lsəʊ / 1
- **alternative** / ɔ:lˈtɜ:nətɪv / 13
- **ambassador** / æmˈbæsədə^{r} / 15
- **ambition** / æmˈbɪʃən / 5
- **angry** / ˈæŋgri / 9
- **ankle** / ˈæŋkəl / 8
- **anywhere** / ˈeniweə^{r} / 14
- **apologise** / əˈpɒlədʒaɪz / *v* TP
- **apology** / əˈpɒlədʒi / 14
- **appointment** / əˈpɔɪntmənt / 12
- **arena** / əˈri:nə / 2
- **argue** / ˈɑ:gju: / *v* 13
- **argument** / ˈɑ:gjʊmənt / 16
- **army** / ˈɑ:mi / 11
- **around** / əˈraʊnd / 4
- **arrange** / əˈreɪndʒ / *v* 8
- **arrive** / əˈraɪv /: **arr.** (*abbrev.*) 8
- **artist** / ɑ:ˈtɪst / 6
- **assembly-line** / əˈsembli laɪn / 4
  - **assembly-line worker** 4
- **astonished** / əˈstɒnɪʃt / 9
- **at: at last** / ət ˈlɑ:st / 1
- **Athens** / ˈæθɪnz / 4
- **athlete** / ˈæθli:t / 9
- **Atlantic** / ətˈlæntɪk / 8
- **atomic** / əˈtɒmɪk / 13
- **attack** / əˈtæk /: **heart attack** 12
- **attractive** / əˈtræktɪv / 1
- **automatic** / ˌɔ:təˈmætɪk / 3
- **award** / əˈwɔ:d / 15

B

- **baby** / ˈbeɪbi / 9
- **babysit** / ˈbeɪbisɪt / *v* 2
- **back** / bæk / *n* 12
- **back** / bæk /: **pay back** 7
- **bad** / bæd / 4
- **badly** / ˈbædli / 13
- **bald** / bɔ:ld / 1
- **ball** / bɔ:l / 1
- **bar** / bɑ:^{r} / *n* 2
- **bargain** / ˈbɑ:gən / 6
- **base** / beɪs / *v* 2
- **basement** / ˈbeɪsmənt / 6
- **bath** / bɑ:θ / 8
- **bay** / beɪ / 10
- **be: be careful** / bɪ ˈkeəfəl / 11
- **beard** / bɪəd / *n* 1
- **beat** / bi:t / *v* 14
- **beautiful** / ˈbju:tɪfəl / 1
- **become** / bɪˈkʌm / 13
- **bee** / bi: / 16
- **beer** / bɪə^{r} / 12
- **begin** / bɪˈgɪn / *v* 1
- **belong to** / bɪˈlɒŋ tʊ / 11
- **below** / bɪˈləʊ / 7
  - **below zero** 7
- **bench** / bentʃ / 14
- **bend** / bend / *n* 9
- **bend** / bend / *v* 15
- **Ben Nevis** / ben ˈnevɪs / 5
- **best** / best / 5
- **better** / ˈbetə^{r} / 3
- **big: bigger** / ˈbɪgə^{r} / 3
- **bike** (**bicycle**) / baɪk / 4
- **binoculars** / bɪˈnɒkjʊləz / 1
- **birthday** / ˈbɜ:θdeɪ / 7
- **bistro** / ˈbi:strəʊ / 2
- **bit: a bit** / əˈbɪt / 14
- **bite** / baɪt / *v* 14
- **blow** / bləʊ *v* 15
- **board** / bɔ:d /: **Electricity Board** 14
- **boat** / bəʊt /: **sailing boat** 15
- **bomb** / bɒm / 11
- **bored** / ˈbɔ:d / **be/get bored** 4
- **boring** / ˈbɔ:rɪŋ / *adj* 4
- **both** / bəʊθ / 2
- **box** / bɒks /: **boxing** 2
- **break** / breɪk / *v* 8
  - **break out** (fire) 1
  - **break down** 8
  - **break open** 13
- **breathe** / bri:ð / *v* 13
- **bright: brighter** / ˈbraɪtə^{r} / 7
- **Brighton** / ˈbraɪtən / 2
- **British** / ˈbrɪtɪʃ / 15
  - **British Rail** 8
- **broken-hearted** / ˌbrəʊkənˈhɑ:tɪd / 15
- **brown** / braʊn / 10
- **build** / bɪld / *v* 11
- **bus** / bʌs /: **bus stop** 7
- **business** / ˈbɪznɪs / 8
  - **Business Studies** TP
- **businessman** / ˈbɪznɪsmən / 15
- **busy** / ˈbɪzi / 11
- **by** / baɪ / 5
  - **by cheque** 5
  - **by mistake** 11
  - **by the way** 7

C

- **calm** / kɑ:m / 9
  - **calm down** *v* 14
- **cancer** / ˈkænsə^{r} / 13
- **captain** / ˈkæptɪn / 9
- **care** / keə^{r} / 16
- **career** / kəˈrɪə^{r} / 9
- **careful** / ˈkeəfəl / 11
  - **be careful** 11
- **carpenter** / kɑ:pəntə^{r} / 13
- **carry** / ˈkæri /: **carry out** 11
- **cassette radio player** / kəˌset ˈreɪdɪəʊ ˌpleɪə^{r} / 5
- **catch** / kætʃ / *v* 8
  - **catch fire** 9
  - **catch up** 14
- **cause** / kɔ:z / *v* 11
- **central** / ˈsentrəl /: **central heating** 6
- **century** / ˈsentʃəri / 15
- **ceremony** / ˈserɪməni / 15
- **certain** / ˈsɜ:tn /: **certainly** 5
- **chance** / tʃɑ:ns / *n* 7
- **change** / tʃeɪndʒ / *v* 4
- **charge** / tʃɑ:dʒ / 10
- **charming** / ˈtʃɑ:mɪŋ / 6
- **cheap: cheaper** / ˈtʃi:pə^{r} / 3
- **cheapest** / ˈtʃi:pɪst / 5
- **check** / tʃek / *v* 10
  - **check out** *v* 8
- **check-in** / ˈtʃek ɪn / *adj* 8
- **cheer** / ˈtʃɪə^{r} / *v* 9
- **cheesecake** / ˈtʃi:zkeɪk / 10
- **chemist** / ˈkemɪst / 12
- **cheque** / tʃek / 5
- **chess** / tʃes / 5
- **children** / ˈtʃɪldrən / 2
- **chimpanzee** / ˌtʃɪmpænˈzi: / 3
- **China** / ˈtʃaɪnə / 13
- **Chinese** / ˌtfaɪˈni:z / 12
- **Christmas** / ˈkrismәs / 8
- **chop** / tʃɒp /: **lamb chop** 10
- **cider** / ˈsaɪdə^{r} / 10
- **cigar: cigar-shaped** / sɪˈgɑ:sheɪpt / 1
- **classical** / ˈklæsɪkəl / *adj* 2
- **clean** / kli:n / *adj* 4
- **cleaner** / ˈkli:nə^{r} / *adj* 6
- **clear** / klɪə^{r} / 3
- **clearly** / ˈklɪəli / 13
- **close to** / ˈkləʊs tʊ / *adv* 2
- **cloudy** / ˈklaʊdi / 7
- **clove** (**of garlic**) / kləʊv / 10
- **coal** / kəʊl / 13
- **coast** / kəʊst / 6
- **cold** / kəʊld / *n* 7
- **college** / ˈkɒlɪdʒ / 2
  - **technical college** 2
- **colour** / ˈkʌlə^{r} / *adj* 5
  - **colour television** 5
- **come** / kʌm /: **come down** 11
  - **come out** 9
- **comfortable** / ˈkʌmftəbəl / 14
- **comfortably** / ˈkʌmftəbli / 11
- **companion** / kəmˈpænɪən / 10
- **company** / ˈkʌmpəni / 1
- **compare** / kəmˈpeə^{r} / *v* 5
- **complaint** / kəmˈpleɪnt / 5
- **complete** / kəmˈpli:t / *adj* 6
- **completely** / kəmˈpli:tli / 12
- **compliment** / ˈkɒmplɪmənt / *v* 9
- **comprehension** / ˌkɒmprɪˈhenʃən / 2
- **computer** / kəmˈpju:tə^{r} / 1
- **conditional** / kənˈdɪʃənəl / 16
- **conditions** / kənˈdɪʃənz / 4
- **congratulations** / kənˈgrætʃʊˈleɪʃənz / 16
- **cons** / kɒnz / (*abbrev. for* **conveniences**) 6
  - **mod cons** / mɒd kɒnz / 6
- **conservation** / ˌkɒnsəˈveɪʃən / 13
- **conservative** / kənˈsɜ:vətɪv / *adj* 4
- **conserve** / kənˈsɜ:v / *v* 13
- **contain** / kənˈteɪn / *v* 13
- **contest** / ˈkɒntest / *n* 5
- **contestant** / kənˈtestənt / 5
- **control** / kənˈtrəʊl /*n*: **tone control** 5
- **cooking** / ˈkʊkɪŋ / 5
- **correct** / kəˈrekt / *v* 14
- **cosmetics** / kɒzˈmetɪks / 5
- **cost** / kɒst / *v* 3
- **cottage** / ˈkɒtɪdʒ / 6
- **couch** / kaʊtʃ / 12
- **cough** / kɒf / *v* 13
- **could** / kʊd / 3
- **course** (of meal) / kɔ:s / *n* 2
- **crawl** / krɔ:l / *v* 8
- **crew** / kru: / 9
- **crowd** / kraʊd / 8
- **crowded** / kraʊdɪd / 10
- **cube** / kju:b /: **stock cube** 10
- **curly** / ˈkɜ:li / *adj* 1
- **customer** / ˈkʌstəmə^{r} / 3
- **cut** / kʌt / *v* 10
- **cycle** / ˈsaɪkəl / *v* 12
- **cycling** / ˈsaɪklɪŋ / 12

D

- **dancer** / ˈdɑ:nsə^{r} / 1
- **dangerous** / ˈdeɪndʒərəs / 2
- **dangerously** / ˈdeɪndʒərəsli / 13
- **dark** / dɑ:k / *adj* 1
- **dead** / ded /: **drop dead** 14
- **deal** / di:l / *n* 2
  - **a great deal** 13
- **decide** / dɪˈsaɪd / *v* 4
- **decimal** / ˈdesɪməl /: **decimal point** 14
- **decision** / dɪˈsɪʒən / 16
- **decorate** / ˈdekəreɪt / *v* 11
- **deep** / di:p / 11
- **deeply** / ˈdi:pli / 15
- **definite** / ˈdefənɪt / 12
- **degree** / dɪˈgri: / 7
- **delay** / dɪˈleɪ / *v* 8
- **delicious** / dɪˈlɪʃəs / 10
- **deliver** / dɪˈlɪvə^{r} / *v* 5
- **delivery** / dɪˈlɪvəri / 4

de luxe / dɪ ˈlʌks / 3
demonstration / ˌdemənˈstreɪʃən / 13
demonstrator / ˈdemənstreɪtə^{r} / 13
depart / dɪˈpɑːt /: **dep.** (*abbrev.*) *v* 8
department / dɪˈpɑːtmənt / 2
department store 5
depend / dɪˈpend / *v* 5
depend on *v* 4
describe / dɪˈskraɪb / *v* 1
description / dɪˈskrɪpʃən / 1
desk / desk /: **check-in desk** 8
diamond / ˈdaɪəmənd / *n* 3
difference / ˈdɪfərəns / 8
difficult / ˈdɪfɪkəlt / 3
dig / dɪg / *v* 13
dining room / ˈdaɪnɪŋ rʊm / 6
direct / dɪˈrekt, daɪ- / *adj* 11
director / dɪˈrektə^{r}, daɪ- / 1
dirty / ˈdɜːti / *adj* 4
disagree / ˌdɪsəˈgriː / 13
disappoint / ˌdɪsəˈpɔɪnt / *v* 9
disastrous / dɪˈzɑːstrəs / *adj* 15
discount / dɪsˈkaʊnt / 5
discuss / dɪˈskʌs / *v* 2
dish / dɪʃ / 10
Disneyland / ˈdɪsnɪlænd / 8
distance / ˈdɪstəns / 12
diver / ˈdaɪvə^{r} / 4
doctor / ˈdɒktə^{r} / 12
dog / dɒg / 6
Dorset / ˈdɔːsɪt / 10
doubt / daʊt / *v* 15
downstairs / ˌdaʊnˈsteəz / 6
drama / drɑːmə / 15
dressing / ˈdresɪŋ / *n* 10
drop / drɒp / *v* 11
drop dead *v* 14
drown / draʊn / 15
drunk / ˈdrʌŋk / 4
dry / draɪ / (opp. **wet**) 7
dry / draɪ / (opp. **sweet**) 10
duchess / ˈdʌtʃɪs / 15
due / djuː / 8
during / ˈdjʊərɪŋ / 9
dust / dʌst / 13

E

each / iːtʃ / 5
ear(s) / ɪə^{r}; ɪəz / 1
early: earlier / ˈɜːlɪə^{r} / 9
east / iːst / 7
eastern / ˈiːstən / 7
easy: easier / ˈiːsɪə^{r} / 3
echo / ˈekəʊ / 15
electric / ɪˈlektrɪk / *adj* 9
electricity / ɪˌlekˈtrɪsɪti / 14
Electricity Board 14
electronics / ɪˌlekˈtrɒnɪks /: **International Electronics** 1
else / els /: **someone else** 1
emphasise / ˈemfəsaɪz / 15
end / end / *v* 1
energy / ˈenədʒi / 13
engine / ˈendʒɪn / 11
Englishman / ˈɪnglɪʃmən / 9
enjoy / ɪnˈdʒɔɪ / *v* 1
enough /ɪˈnʌf/ 13
entirely / ɪnˈtaɪəli / 13
equal / ˈiːkwəl / 13
error / ˈerə^{r} / 14
Europe / ˈjʊərəp / 9
even / iːvən / 2
everyone / ˈevriwʌn / 7
everything / ˈevriθɪŋ / 7
everywhere / ˈevriweə^{r} / 6
exact / ɪgˈzækt / 15
exam / ɪgˈzæm / (*abbrev. for* **examination**) 2
examine / ɪgˈzæmɪn / *v* 12
example / ɪgˈzɑːmpəl /: **for example** 4
excellent / ˈeksələnt / 11
except / ɪkˈsept / 7
exciting / ɪkˈsaɪtɪŋ / 9
exercise / ˈeksəsaɪz / *n* 5
expense / ɪkˈspens /: **expense account** 12
experience / ɪkˈspɪərɪəns / 4
expert / ˈekspɜːt / 8
explain / ɪkˈspleɪn/ *v* 1
explode / ɪkˈspləʊd / *v* 11
explosion / ɪkˈspləʊʒən / 13
export / ˈekspɔːt / *n* 4
express / ɪkˈspres / 15
extra / ˈekstrə / 4
eye(s) / aɪ; aɪz / 1

F

fact / fækt /: **in fact** 7
fail / feɪl / *v* 14
faint / feɪnt / *v* 15
fair / feə^{r} / *adj* 1
fair / feə^{r} /: **it isn't fair** 4
fall / fɔːl / *v* 1
fall into 1
fall in love 9
family / ˈfæməli / 12
famous / ˈfeɪməs / 1
fancy / ˈfænsi / 10
far / fɑː^{r} / 14
fast / fɑːst / 5
fat / fæt / 1
fault / fɔːlt / 9
favourite / ˈfeɪvərɪt / *adj* 2
fear / fɪə^{r} / 14
feel / fiːl / *v* 9
festival / ˈfestɪvəl / 15
few / fjuː / 2
field / fiːld / *n* 1
fight / faɪt / *n* 13
fight / faɪt / *v* 5
figure / ˈfɪgə^{r} / 10
fill / fɪl / *v* 12
film / fɪlm /: **film star** 1
filter / ˈfɪltə^{r} / *n* 13
final / ˈfaɪnəl / *adj* 5
finally / ˈfaɪnəli / 8
finger(s) / ˈfɪŋgə^{r}; ˈfɪŋgəz / 11
finish / ˈfɪnɪʃ / *n* 9
fire (dismiss) / faɪə^{r} / *v* 4
fire / faɪə^{r} /: **catch fire** *v* 9
first / fɜːst /: **at first** 1
fit / fɪt / 12
get fit 12
keep fit 12
flame / fleɪm / *n* 10
flash / flæʃ / 15
flat / flæt / *adj* 1
floating / ˈfləʊtɪŋ / 8
flute / fluːt / 2
flying saucer / ˌflaɪ-ɪŋ ˈsɔːsə^{r} / 1
focus / fəʊkəs / 1
folk / fəʊk / *adj* 2
fool / fuːl / 15
foot / fʊt /: **on foot** 8
football / ˈfʊtbɔːl / 2
football match 2
football pools 3
forehead / ˈfɒrəd, ˈfɔːhed / 1
foreigner / ˈfɒrənə^{r} / 8
forest / ˈfɒrɪst / 13
forget / fəˈget / 7
form / fɔːm / *n* 6
forward / ˈfɔːwəd / TP
look forward to TP
France / frɑːns / 8
free: freely / ˈfriːli / 13
freezing / ˈfriːzɪŋ / 7
frequent / ˈfriːkwənt / 6
fresh /freʃ / 7
friendly / ˈfrendli / 6
frost / frɒst / 7
fry / fraɪ / 10
full / fʊl /: **fully** 3
in full 6
fun / fʌn / 2
furious / ˈfjʊərɪəs / 9
furnished / ˈfɜːnɪʃt / 6
future / ˈfjuːtʃə^{r} / 9

G

gang / gæŋ / *n* 1
garden / ˈgɑːdn / 6
gardening / ˈgɑːdnɪŋ / 5
garlic / ˈgɑːlɪk / 10
gas / gæs / 6
gather / ˈgæðə^{r} / 13
general / ˈdʒenərəl / *adj* 2
gerund / ˈdʒerənd / 2
get / get /: **get down** 8
get fit 12
glad / glæd / 14
glass / glɑːs / 12
glasses / ˈglɑːsɪz / 14
go / gəʊ /: **go down** 11
go off 11
go to 2
go up 1
goal / gəʊl / 2
gold / gəʊld / *adj* 3
good / gʊd /: **Good Lord!** 10
good luck 16
gorilla / gəˈrɪlə / 3
government / ˈgʌvəmənt / 13
grease / griːs / 4
great / greɪt / (=**splendid**) 9
groan / grəʊn / *v* 12
ground / graʊnd / *n* 2
group / gruːp / *n* 2
guess / ges / *v* 12
guided / ˈgaɪdɪd /: **guided tour** 8
guitarist / gɪˈtɑːrɪst / 2
gullible / ˈgʌləbəl /: **Dr Gullible** 15
gymnastics / dʒɪmˈnæstɪks / 5

H

hair / heə^{r} / 1
hand(s) / hænd; hændz /: **hands up!** 3
on the other hand 12
handsome / ˈhænsəm / 1
happy: happier / ˈhæpɪə^{r} / 5
harbour / ˈhɑːbə^{r} / 15
hard / hɑːd / *adj* 4
hate / heɪt / *v* 2
head / hed / 1
headline / ˈhedlaɪn / 1
health / helθ / 12
heart / hɑːt / 11
heart attack 12
broken-hearted 15
heart-transplant 11
heat / hiːt / *v* 13
heater / ˈhiːtə^{r} / 9
heating / ˈhiːtɪŋ /: **central heating** 6
heavy / ˈhevi / 5
heavily / ˈhevɪli / 13
height / haɪt / 5
helicopter / ˈhelɪkɒptə^{r} / 11
helper / ˈhelpə^{r} / 4
herb / hɜːb / 10
hey! / heɪ / 11
high: higher / ˈhaɪə^{r} / 5
hire / haɪə^{r} / *v* 4
hit / hɪt / *v* 4
hobby / ˈhɒbi / 2
hole / həʊl / 11
holiday / hɒlədi / 2
Hollywood / ˈhɒliwʊd / 9
home / həʊm /: **home-made** 10
homesick 6
homework 12
honest / ˈɒnɪst / 10
honeymoon / ˈhʌnimuːn / 9
Hong Kong / hɒŋ ˈkɒŋ / 4
hope / həʊp / *n* 14
hospital / ˈhɒspɪtl / 4
hot / hɒt / 10
housewife / ˈhaʊs-waɪf / 12
Hove / həʊv / 8
however / haʊˈevə^{r} / 15
huge / hjuːdʒ / 14
hundreds / ˈhʌndrədz / 6
hurt / hɜːt / *v* 12

I

ice / aɪs / 7
identification / aɪˌdentɪfɪˈkeɪʃən / 7

idiot / 'ɪdɪət / 13
ill / ɪl / 4
illness / 'ɪlnɪs / 13
important / ɪm'pɔ:tənt / 2
in: in fact / ɪn 'fækt / 7
include / ɪn'klu:d / 8
industry / 'ɪndəstri / 6
infinitive / ɪn'fɪnɪtɪv / 2
ingredients / ɪn'gri:dɪənts / 10
inside / ɪn'saɪd / 6
instead / ɪn'sted / 7
instrument / 'ɪnstrəmənt / 2
intend / ɪn'tend / *v* 6
intention / ɪn'tenʃən / 9
interest / 'ɪntrəst / *n* 5
international / ˌɪntə'næʃənəl / 1
  International Electronics 1
interviewer / 'ɪntəvju:ə^{r} / 4
introduce / ˌɪntrə'dju:s / *v* TP
Inverness / ˌɪnvə'nes / 6
investigate / ɪn'vestɪgeɪt / *v* 1
invite / ɪn'vaɪt / *v* TP
irregular / ɪ'regjʊlə^{r} / 14
Italy / 'ɪtəli / 8
its / ɪts / 1

J

jail / dʒeɪl / *n* 13
jam / dʒæm / (traffic) *n* 8
  jammed / dʒæmd / 8
Japanese (language) / ˌdʒæpə'ni:z / 15
jewel / 'dʒu:əl / 11
jog / dʒɒg / *v* 5
jogging / 'dʒɒgɪŋ / 12
juice / dʒu:s / 10
jumbo / 'dʒʌmbəʊ / *adj* 15
jump / dʒʌmp /: **jump down** 15
  jump off 15
just / dʒʌst / 1

K

keep / ki:p / 8
  keep fit 12
kick / kɪk / *v* 11
kidnapper / 'kɪdnæpə^{r} / 1
kiss / kɪs / *v* 16
knock / nɒk /: **knock down** 7
knock / nɒk / *n* 15

L

label / 'leɪbəl / 10
lake / leɪk / 13
lamb / læm /: **lamb chop** 10
land / lænd / *v* 1
language / 'læŋgwɪdʒ /: **language school** 6
large / lɑ:dʒ / 6
last / lɑ:st / *v* 7
lately / 'leɪtli / 9
latest / 'leɪtɪst / 11
lead / li:d / *v* 11
lead / li:d / *n* 9
leader / li:də^{r} / 9
leaf/leaves / li:f, li:vz / 10
least / li:st /: **at least** 9
left over / left 'əʊvə^{r} / 13
lemon / 'lemən / 10
lend / lend / *v* 14
lie (in) / laɪ / *v* 2
  lie across 15
lie (tell untruths) / laɪ / *v* 7
lie / laɪ / *n* 7
life / laɪf / 3
  pl. **lives** / laɪvz / 15
light / laɪt / *v* 13
lightning / 'laɪtnɪŋ / 9
line (railway) / laɪn / 15
litre / 'li:tə^{r} / 10
little / 'lɪtl / 3
living / 'lɪvɪŋ / 5
load / ləʊd / *n* 13
local / 'ləʊkəl / *adj* 13
lonely / 'ləʊnli / 6
look / lʊk /
  look forward to TP
  look like 1
  look round 9
look / lʊk / *n* 11
lord / lɔ:d /: **Good Lord!** 10
lorry / 'lɒri / 7
lose / lu:z / *v* 2
lot: a lot / ə 'lɒt / 12
love / lʌv / *v* 7
lover / 'lʌvə^{r} / 15
low / ləʊ / 6
luck / lʌk /: **good luck** 16
lucky / 'lʌki / 11
luckily / 'lʌkɪli / 12
lung(s) / lʌŋ, lʌŋz / 13
luxury / 'lʌkʃəri / 6

M

machine / mə'ʃi:n /: **washing machine** 5
main / meɪn / *adj* 5
make / meɪk / *v* 1
management / 'mænɪdʒmənt / 6
many / 'meni /: **not many** 6
march / mɑ:tʃ / *v* 13
marjoram / 'mɑ:dʒərəm / 10
marriage / mærɪdʒ / 1
marry / 'mæri / *v* 1
marvellous / 'mɑ:vələs / 9
Massachusetts / ˌmæsə'tʃu:sɪts / 10
match / mætʃ / *n* 2
  football match 2
mathematics / ˌmæθə'mætɪks / 5
matter / 'mætə^{r} /: **doesn't matter** 3
maximum / 'mæksɪməm / 7
may / meɪ / 11
meal / mi:l / 8
mechanic / mɪ'kænɪk / 4
medicine / 'medsən / 13
medium / 'mi:dɪəm / *adj* 10
medium-sized / 'mi:dɪəm-saɪzd / 6
meeting / 'mi:tɪŋ / 8
memory / 'meməri / 7
mention / 'menʃən / *v* 12
menu / 'menju: / 10
metal / 'metl / 11
metre / 'mi:tə^{r} / 9
middle / 'mɪdl / *n* 1
  middle-aged 1
mile / maɪl / 6
mine / maɪn /: **coal mine** 13
minAum / 'mɪnɪməm / 7
miracle / 'mɪrəkəl / 15
missing / 'mɪsɪŋ / *adj* 1
mistake / mɪ'steɪk / *n* 9
  by mistake 11
modern / 'mɒdn / 5
mod / mɒd / (*abbrev. for* **modern**) / 6
  mod. cons. 6
moon / mu:n / *n* 1
more / mɔ:r /: **even more** 2
most / məʊst / 1
motorway / 'məʊtəweɪ / 6
mountain / 'maʊntən / 5
moustache / mə'stɑ:ʃ / 1
move / mu:v / *n* 9
moving / 'mu:vɪŋ / *adj* 15
Mt Blanc / mɔ̃ 'blɔ̃ / 5
Mt Everest / maʊnt 'evərɪst / 5
much / mʌtʃ /: **much better** 5
  not much 3
museum / mju:'zɪəm / 6
mushroom / 'mʌʃru:m / 10
musical / 'mju:zɪkəl / *n* 9
musician / mju:'zɪʃən / 2
must / mʌst / 3

N

nasty / 'nɑ:sti / 14
naturally / 'nætərəli / 14
near: nearest / 'nɪərɪst / 8
nearby / nɪə'baɪ / 14
necessary / 'nesəsəri / 13
need / ni:d / *v* 3
nervous / nɜ:vəs / 12
nightmare / 'naɪtmeə^{r} / 14
nobody / 'nəʊbədi / 7
noise / nɔɪz / 6
nonsense / 'nɒnsəns / 13
north / nɔ:θ / 6
  north-eastern 7
not / nɒt /: **not many** 5
  why not 5
notes / nəʊts / 8
nothing / 'nʌθɪŋ / 9
notice / 'nəʊtɪs / *v* 4
noun / naʊn / 13
nuclear / 'nju:klɪə^{r} / 13

O

object (thing) / 'ɒbdʒɪkt / *n* 1
ocean / 'əʊʃən / 13
offer / 'ɒfə^{r} / *v* 14
oil / ɔɪl / 1
  olive oil 10
old: older / 'əʊldə^{r} / 3
oldest / 'əʊldɪst / 5
old-fashioned ˌəʊld 'fæʃənd / 5
olive / 'ɒlɪv /: **olive oil** 10
on / ɒn /: **on foot** 8
onion / 'ʌnjən / 10
operation / ˌɒpə'reɪʃən / 11
order / 'ɔ:də^{r} / *v* 1
Oscar / 'ɒskə^{r} / 15
others (of people) / 'ʌðəz / 1
out / aʊt /
  out of breath 12
  point out *v* 13
  run out *v* 13
outlook / 'aʊtlʊk / 7
oven / 'ʌvən / 10
over / 'əʊvə^{r} /: **over here** 2
  over there 1
  left over 13
overcharge / ˌəʊvə'tʃɑ:dʒ / *v* 10
overtime / 'əʊvətaɪm / 4
overweight / 'əʊvəweɪt / 12
own / əʊn / *pron* 2
Oxford Street / 'ɒksfəd stri:t / 3

P

package / 'pækɪdʒ /: **package tour** 8
packet / 'pækɪt / 10
pain / peɪn / 12
painful / 'peɪnfəl / TP
paint / peɪnt / *v* 15
pan / pæn / 10
parachute / 'pærəʃu:t / 2
Paris / 'pærɪs / 6
particularly / pə'tɪkjʊləli / 7
party / 'pɑ:ti / 11
pass / pɑ:s / *v* 9
pass (exams) / pɑ:s / *v* 14
passive (tense) / 'pæsɪv / 11
past / pɑ:st / *n* 4
past (tense) / pɑ:st /
  past progressive 15
patient / 'peɪʃənt / 11
pay / peɪ /: **pay back** 7
  pay by cheque 5
perfect / 'pɜ:fɪkt / *adj* 15
permission / pə'mɪʃən / 10
personality / ˌpɜ:sə'næləti / 5
personnel / ˌpɜ:sə'nel / 4
persuade / pə'sweɪd / *v* 15
pet / pet / 6
petrol / 'petrəl / 9
philosophy / fɪ'lɒsəfi / 5
photographer / fə'tɒgrəfə^{r} / 6
phrasebook / 'freɪzbʊk / 15
Picasso / pɪ'kæsəʊ / 1
picnic / 'pɪknɪk / *n* 2
piece / pi:s / 10
pill / pɪl / 15
pilot / 'paɪlət / 9
pit / pɪt / 13
pity / 'pɪti / 16
place / pleɪs /: **take place** *v* 15
plan / plæn / *n and v* 9
planet / 'plænɪt / 1

tall / tɔ:l / *adj* 1
taller / ˈtɔ:lə^r / 3
tallest / ˈtɔ:lɪst / 5
tank / tæŋk /: **petrol tank** 9
tape / teɪp / 6
taste / teɪst *v* 10
tax / tæks / 8
team / ti:m / 11
technical / ˈteknɪkəl / 2
  technical college 2
teeth / ti:θ / (*pl. of* **tooth**) 14
television / ˈtelɪˌvɪʒən /: **colour television** 5
telly (television) / ˈteli / 7
temperature / ˈtempərətʃə^r / 7
tender / ˈtendə^r / 10
tense / tens / *n* 12
terrified / ˈterɪfaɪd / 9
terrifying / ˈterɪfaɪ-ɪŋ / 9
test / test / 12
than / ðən / 3
that / ðæt /: **that's why** TP
theatre / ˈθɪətə^r / 6
theme / θi:m / 2
there / ðeə^r /: **over there** 1
  there was 1
thin / θɪn / 1
thousands (people) / ˈθaʊsəndz / 1
thrilling / ˈθrɪlɪŋ / 9
through / θru: / *adj* 8
throw / θrəʊ / *v* 13
thunder / ˈθʌndə^r / 15
thyme / taɪm / 10
tidal / ˈtaɪdl / *adj* 13
tide / taɪd / 13
tie / taɪ / *n* 4
time / taɪm /: **this time** 1
  point in time 7
  waste time *v* 15
timetable / ˈtaɪmˌteɪbl / 8
tin / tɪn / 10
tip / tɪp / *n* 4
toe(s) / təʊ; təʊz / 12
together / təˈgeðə^r / 2
tone / təʊn /: **tone control** 5
too / tu: /: **too much** 8
top / tɒp / 12
touch / tʌtʃ / *v* 12
tough / tʌf / 10
tour / tʊə^r /*n*: **guided tour** 8
  package tour 8
tourist / ˈtʊərɪst / 6
towards / təˈwɔ:dz / 8
traffic / ˈtræfɪk /: **traffic jam** 7
tragic / ˈtrædʒɪk / 15
trainee / treɪˈni: / 8
transplant / ˈtrænsplɑ:nt /: **heart-transplant** 11
transport / ˈtrænspɔ:t /: **public transport** 7
trap / træp / *v* 15
travel / ˈtrævəl / *v* 4
travel / ˈtrævəl / *n* 7
traveller / ˈtrævələ^r / 8
Trinidad / ˈtrɪnɪdæd / 2
trouble / ˈtrʌbəl / 8
trousers / ˈtraʊzəz / 12
true / tru: / *adj* 3
truth / tru:θ / 7
try / traɪ / *v* 10
tunnel / ˈtʌnl / 15
turn / tɜ:n /: **turn back** 9

U

ugh! / ʊx, ʌg / 10
ugly / ˈʌgli / 1
uncle / ˈʌŋkəl / 13
underground / ˈʌndəgraʊnd / 8
United States / juˌnaɪtɪd ˈsteɪts / 3
unnecessary / ʌnˈnesəsəri / 13
unreal / ˌʌnrɪəl / 16
unsafe / ʌnseɪf / 13
until / ʌnˈtɪl / 8
unusual / ʌnˈju:ʒʊəl / 9
up / ʌp /: **go up** 1
  hands up! 3
upset / ʌpˈset / 14
upstairs / ˌʌpˈsteəz / 6
used to / ˈju:st tə / *v* 9

V

value / ˈvælju: / 10
vegetarian / ˌvedʒəˈteərɪən / 2
Viet Nam / ˌvɪət ˈnæm / 1
view / vju: / *n* 6
village / ˈvɪlɪdʒ / 6
visit / ˈvɪzɪt / *v* 6
voice / vɔɪs / 1
vote / vəʊt / *v* 15
vs / ˈvɜ:səs / (*abbrev. for* **versus**) 2

W

waitress / ˈweɪtrəs / 4
wall / wɔ:l / 6
war / wɔ:^{r} /: **Second World War** 16
  World War II 11
war-time / ˈwɔ:taɪm / *adj* 16
washing machine / ˈwɒʃɪŋ məˌʃi:n / 5
waste / weɪst / *n* 13
waste / weɪst /: **waste time** 15
watch /wɒtʃ / *n* 3
waterproof / ˈwɔ:təpru:f / 3
wave / weɪv / *n* 13
wave / weɪv / *v* 15
way / weɪ / 1
  by the way 7
weather / ˈweðə^r / *n* 4
weatherman / ˈweðəmæn / 7
weekend / ˌwi:kˈend / 2
weight / weɪt / 5
well done / ˌwellˈdʌn / 10
west / west / 7
wet / wet / 14
whistle / ˈwɪsəl / 16
whole / həʊl / 10
why / waɪ /: **that's why** TP
will / wɪl / *v* 7
widow / ˈwɪdəʊ / 3
wildly / ˈwaɪldli / 9
win / wɪn / *v* 2
wind / wɪnd / *n* 2
windy / ˈwɪndi / 7
winter / ˈwɪntə^r / 8
without / wɪˈðaʊt / 7
wonder / ˈwʌndə^r / *v* 8
wood / wʊd / 5
work / wɜ:k / *n* 6
worker / ˈwɜ:kə^r / 4
  assembly-line worker 4
world / wɜ:ld / 3
worry / ˈwʌri /: **don't worry** 7
worse/worst / wɜ:s, wɜ:st / 5
worth / wɜ:θ / 11
would / wʊd / 2
writing / ˈraɪtɪŋ / 14

X Y Z

X-ray / ˈeks reɪ / *n* 12
yoga / ˈjəʊgə / 5
younger / ˈjʌŋgə^r / 3
youngest / ˈjʌŋgɪst / 5
yourself / jəˈself / 16
zero / ˈzɪərəʊ /: **below zero** 7

For teachers in Spain:

Autorizado por el Ministerio de Educación y Ciencia con fecha 1.12.83 (B.O.E. 17.1.84)